I0057061

Buying Online Businesses The Warren Buffett Way

The Value Investing Strategy to Building Wealth with Little Money

Hyun Kim CFA

Copyright © 2025 by Hyun Kim, CFA

All rights reserved.

No portion of this book may be reproduced in any form without written permission from the publisher or author, except as permitted by U.S. copyright law.

This publication is designed to provide accurate and authoritative information in regard to the subject matter covered. It is sold with the understanding that neither the author nor the publisher is engaged in rendering legal, investment, accounting or other professional services. While the publisher and author have used their best efforts in preparing this book, they make no representations or warranties with respect to the accuracy or completeness of the contents of this book and specifically disclaim any implied warranties of merchantability or fitness for a particular purpose. No warranty may be created or extended by sales representatives or written sales materials. The advice and strategies contained herein may not be suitable for your situation. You should consult with a professional when appropriate. Neither the publisher nor the author shall be liable for any loss of profit or any other commercial damages, including but not limited to special, incidental, consequential, personal, or other damages.

Disclaimer

The information provided in this book is for informational purposes only and is not intended to be a source of investment and financial advice or analysis with respect to the material presented. The information and/or documents contained in this book do not constitute legal or financial advice and should never be used without first consulting with a financial professional to determine what may be best for your individual needs.

The publisher and the author do not make any guarantee or other promise as to any results that may be obtained from using the content of this book. You should never make any investment decision without first consulting with your own financial advisor and conducting your own research and due diligence. To the maximum extent permitted by law, the publisher and the author disclaim any and all liability in the event any information, commentary,analysis, opinions, advice and/or recommendations contained in this book prove to be inaccurate, incomplete or unreliable, or result in any investment or other losses.

Content contained or made available through this book is not intended to and does not constitute legal advice or investment advice and no attorney-client relationship is formed. The publisher and the author are providing this book and its contents on an "as is" basis. Your use of the information in this book is at your own risk.

Contents

Introduction: One Big Shift by Buffett

Imagine a portfolio filled with great businesses, some public stocks, some private companies, all compounding quietly in the background, just like Warren Buffett has at Berkshire Hathaway. Sounds like a billionaire's playground, right?

Most people hear that and think, "Well, that's nice if you've got a few hundred million lying around." But the truth is, you don't need Buffett's wallet to borrow his playbook. You just need to adopt his mindset, one focused on owning great businesses, not just trading stocks.

Here's where it gets interesting. If you know where to look and learn how to spot quality, you can buy small but mighty online businesses for a few thousand dollars. We're talking less than what most people spend upgrading their phone every couple of years. But instead of getting a new screen to scroll, you're buying an income stream. A real business. Something that puts you in the driver's seat.

When you own a business, even a tiny one, everything changes. You're not just betting on the next earnings call. You're collecting cash flow. You're calling the shots. You're learning how to build value the old-fashioned way: by serving customers, improving operations, and thinking long term.

That's how you build your own version of a Berkshire portfolio. It might start small, maybe with just a Shopify store, a content site, or a niche SaaS app, but the principles are timeless. Buy good businesses. Don't overpay. Let compounding do the heavy lifting.

And if you're willing to be patient, keep learning, and play the long game, you'll be surprised how fast that snowball can grow.

As Buffett once said, "I always knew I was going to be rich. I don't think I ever doubted it for a minute." You don't need to say it out loud. But if you start thinking like an owner and acting like one, you're already on the right path.

My Journey

My son's name is Warren. And yes, it's exactly who you're thinking: Warren Buffett.

I didn't name him that just because I admire the man, though I do. I named him Warren because I wanted my son to grow up with a set of values that matter, not just in business, but in life.

Things like long-term thinking in a world that chases shortcuts. The discipline to do the right thing even when no one's watching. The integrity to treat people fairly. And maybe most important of all, the understanding that real wealth doesn't come from luck or hype. It comes from owning great businesses and letting time work its magic.

Buffett once said, "The chains of habit are too light to be felt until they are too heavy to be broken." I figure if my son can build the right habits early, ones rooted in patience, curiosity, and character, then he's already ahead of the game.

The name is just a reminder. The values are the real legacy.

Over the years, I've quietly built a portfolio of small online businesses, one deal at a time, mostly during nights and weekends, all while climbing the ladder at a Fortune 500 financial firm in New York. Today, I lead a global team there. It's the kind of job that demands a lot: early mornings, late calls, constant pressure.

And yet, I've found a way to show up consistently, not just at work, but at home. My family still gets the best of me, not the leftovers. That balance hasn't been easy, but it's been worth it. Because for me, building wealth was never about choosing between career and ownership. It was about learning how to do both thoughtfully, patiently, and with a long-term view.

That's the same approach I bring to investing. Slow is smooth. Smooth is fast.

People often ask how I pulled that off. How did I build and manage multiple businesses while working full-time and staying present at home?

The answer is surprisingly simple: outsourcing and automation. That's the core of my strategy, and it's what this book is all about.

Here's what I believe: you don't need to be a billionaire, or even have a lot of free time, to build your own version of Berkshire Hathaway. If you don't have time, use your money to build systems and bring in help. If you don't have money, invest your time to learn, build, and grow from the ground up. That's exactly what I did. And if I can do it, so can you.

Aha Eureka Moment

Every year, I tune in to the day-long Berkshire Hathaway annual meeting. Sometimes live, sometimes watching recordings. What always amazes me isn't just Warren Buffett's wisdom. It's the tens of thousands of people who fly into Omaha, Nebraska, from all over the world just to hear him talk.

You've got long lines, jam-packed stadium seating, and grown adults taking notes like they're back in college. All to hear an elderly man from a small Midwestern town explain, in plain English, how he thinks about investing.

And every time I watch, I find myself wondering:If tens of thousands of people are trying to follow Buffett's principles, do I really have a shot at outperforming them in the stock market?

Surprisingly, the answer is yes, especially if you know where to look.

Decades ago, I started in the stock market like most people do, buying individual stocks, mostly small caps. I liked the idea that in the less-followed corners of the market, my research might actually give me an edge. And it did. I still allocate a meaningful part of my portfolio there.

But here's what changed the game for me: I realized the better odds, the real mis-priced opportunities, might hide outside the stock market.

In private markets, especially with small online businesses, there's no Bloomberg terminal flashing valuations. No analyst reports or hedge funds bidding up prices. It's just you, the seller, and your ability to spot quality and think long term.

That's where I found my unfair advantage. And I believe that's where more investors should start looking if they really want to invest like Buffett.

The stock market is crowded. Competitive. Generally, Efficient most of the time. It's filled with Ivy League fund managers, institutional money, algorithms, and armies of analysts. Everyone is reading the same books and following the same Buffett quotes.

But in the world of private online business acquisitions? It's a different game. Fewer players. Less efficiency. Less institutional capital. More room for mis-pricing. In short: more opportunity.

Before I walk you through this space, I want to back up a bit. Let's look at how Buffett became so successful, and, more importantly, how he evolved as an investor.

One Big Shift from Warren Buffett

In the beginning, Warren Buffett followed his mentor, Ben Graham. Graham taught him to find companies trading below their net tangible assets. Stocks that were cheap on paper, even if the business wasn't all that great.

Buffett later called this the cigar butt strategy:

"You pick up a discarded cigar butt off the street. It's soggy and has just one puff left in it. But hey, it's free, and that last puff is pure profit."

For a while, that worked. Buffett bought deeply undervalued stocks selling far below the net asset value on the book and squeezed out the last bit of value. But over time, he saw the limits of that approach. It wasn't scalable. It wasn't sustainable. And sometimes, getting that last puff meant liquidating assets and laying off workers, something Buffett wasn't proud of.

The real turning point came when Charlie Munger, his long-time business partner, nudged him in a different direction.

"Charlie shoved me in the direction of not just buying bargains, as Ben Graham had taught me. This was the real impact he had on me. It took a powerful force to move me on from Graham's limiting views." — Warren Buffett

"We realized that some company that was selling at two or three times book value could still be a hell of a bargain... sometimes combined with an unusual managerial skill plainly present in some individual or system." — Charlie Munger

This shift from focusing solely on undervalued assets to buying great businesses at fair prices is what made him the Buffett that we see today.

He started buying companies like Coca-Cola, American Express, and See's Candies. These were businesses with brand, pricing power, and durable competitive advantages. As he said about Coke, "We intend to hold Coca-Cola forever."

But this mindset shift wasn't easy. Buffett nearly missed See's Candies, one of his all-time best investments, because he was still too anchored in the old framework.

"The family controlling See's wanted $30 million for the business. But I didn't want to pay more than $25 million and wasn't all that enthusiastic even at that figure. (A price that was three times net tangible assets made me gulp.) My misguided caution could have scuttled a terrific purchase."— 2014 Berkshire Hathaway Chairman's Letter

Had Buffett not made that shift, there's a good chance I wouldn't be quoting him today. His evolution as an investor is what set him apart, and that's what got me thinking.

One Big Shift that I Made

If millions of people are following Buffett's principles in the same public market, how do I differentiate myself? What's my edge?

Buffett evolved from Graham's playbook. What if I evolved from Buffett's?

That led me to three options:

1. Buy Berkshire Hathaway stock and ride Buffett's coattails

2. Follow his 13F filings and mimic his stock picks

3. Apply his principles to a different playing field: private online businesses

As you might've guessed (since I'm writing this book), I went with option three.

But before we go there, let's quickly talk about why the first two options didn't feel quite right for me.

Why I Didn't Choose Option 1 or 2

One approach is to just buy Berkshire Hathaway stock. It's simple, passive, and, let's be honest, hard to argue with. Buffett's track record is legendary for a reason. From 1965 to 2024, the stock compounded at nearly 20% annually. The S&P 500 during that same time? About 10.4%. That kind of long-term outperformance is nothing short of astonishing.

If all you want is a safe, hands-off way to grow your money over time, this strategy makes sense. You're riding shotgun with the greatest investor of all time.

But here's where the shine fades a little. Buffett isn't working with a small fund anymore. He's managing hundreds of billions of dollars, which makes it nearly impossible to find the kind of small, mis-priced opportunities that helped him generate those early, outsized returns. The sheer size of Berkshire Hathaway limits what he can do today.

And then there's the other reality: he's over 90 years old. As much as we'd love for him to run Berkshire forever, no one beats time. The company will carry on, but Buffett's unique touch won't last forever.

That leads to another popular strategy: follow Buffett's 13F filings, the quarterly reports that show what stocks he (or Berkshire) is buying. On paper, it sounds great. Let him do the hard work, and you just mirror his portfolio.

But there's a catch.

Actually, a few.

First, not every investment in the 13F comes from Buffett himself. His lieutenants, Todd and Ted, manage a good portion of the portfolio now. And you don't know which picks came from whom.

Second, the filings are delayed. You're always looking in the rearview mirror. By the time you see what he bought, the price may have already moved. The margin of safety may be gone.

And then there's the part that stung me personally: Buffett can change his mind and sell, and you'll never know why. I once followed a 13F and bought IBM after seeing it show up in Berkshire's holdings. A few months later, I found out Buffett had exited the position entirely. I was left holding the bag, wondering what I'd missed.

The Better Option: My One Big Shift

In the end, I chose a different path. The third one.

I took Buffett's principles, the real ones, and apply them somewhere he hasn't played much: small, profitable online businesses.

It's my version of Buffett's evolution. Just like he moved beyond Ben Graham's strict deep-value approach and started buying high-quality companies with durable moats. I'm taking the next step, moving from public markets to private deals. The principles stay the same. But the game is quieter. The competition is thinner. And the odds of finding mis-priced assets? Much better.

This book is the story of that shift.

It's about taking ideas like circle of competence, margin of safety, moats, and intrinsic value, and putting them to work in a market where you're not competing with thousands of hedge funds and AI-driven models.

You're competing with a solo operator who just wants to sell his website and move on.

This is where I've found the best opportunities of my investing career, and where you might find yours, too.

Let's start the journey together.

Chapter One

Why Private Online Businesses Beat Wall Street

E VERY INVESTOR IS LOOKING for an edge. The one thing that gives them a shot at earning more than the crowd.

The challenge with the stock market today is that the crowd has gotten really smart. You're not just competing with part-time traders anymore. You're up against Wall Street analysts, billion-dollar hedge funds, and high-speed algorithms that react faster than you can blink.

Now, to be clear, I still invest a good chunk of my own portfolio in the stock market. I believe in it. I trust long-term compounding. But I also know that the room for mis-pricing has gotten smaller. Opportunities still exist, but you have to look harder and move faster, and even then, you're often just riding along with the market, not outthinking it.

That's what led me to start looking elsewhere. Not to abandon Buffett's principles, but to apply them in a less crowded arena. One where the players are fewer, the competition is less intense, and the assets are often misunderstood or overlooked.

That arena? *Private online businesses.*

It's a space most investors haven't considered, and that's exactly why it can work. You don't need to beat the market. You just need to buy a solid business at a fair price and, if you're lucky, grow it a little along the way.

Here's why this space caught my attention and what you should think about before diving in yourself.

Why I Love Online Business Investing

Let's be honest, the reason I shifted into online businesses wasn't because I wanted a hobby. It was because the math made sense. These deals can offer better margins of safety, more control, and surprisingly strong returns, especially if you're willing to think like Buffett and do a little digging.

It Starts with Price, and That's the Edge

Ben Graham once said if you had to boil down the secret of sound investing into three words, it'd be: Margin of Safety. And in the public markets, that's getting harder and harder to find. A stock trading at a P/E under 10? Rare. Everyone's watching. Everything's priced in.

But when I started digging into private online businesses, especially content sites and Amazon KDP portfolios, I noticed something. It wasn't unusual to find solid businesses selling for 2.5x or 3x annual earnings. That's like buying a stock with a 30–40% yield, if the cash flow holds up.

That's the first real advantage in this space. The price-to-value gap is wider. And if you know how to do basic due diligence, you can find income streams that are undervalued by any reasonable metric.

We'll dive into intrinsic value and valuation math later, but here's the takeaway: while the public markets feel crowded and picked over, this corner of the investing world still has room for bargains.

Capital-Light Businesses Are a Beautiful Thing

Buffett has always favored businesses that don't need constant infusions of money simply to survive. He calls them capital-light. And once you understand the idea, it's hard to unsee.

Think about it: the less a business needs to reinvest just to keep the lights on, like in factories, trucks, or fancy equipment, the more of its earnings it can actually keep. That leftover cash can go toward growth, dividends, buybacks or straight into your pocket.

Now, here's where it gets interesting: most online businesses fit that model almost perfectly.

You don't need a warehouse. You don't need retail space. You don't need a fleet of technicians in branded vans. With content sites, digital products, or software tools, you often build once and earn for years. Hosting is cheap. Distribution is global. And if you get the fundamentals right, the margins can be jaw-dropping.

Buffett summarized it well in his 2007 shareholders' letter:

"The worst sort of business is one that grows rapidly, requires significant capital to engender the growth, and then earns little or no money. Think airlines. Here, a durable competitive advantage has proven elusive ever since the days of the Wright Brothers. Indeed, if a farsighted capitalist had been present at Kitty Hawk, he would have done his successors a huge favor by shooting Orville down. The airline industry's demand for capital ever since that first flight has been insatiable. Investors have poured money into a bottomless pit, attracted by growth when they should have been repelled by it."

You Can Grow Without the Growing Pains

Most traditional businesses get harder as they grow. More customers usually mean more headaches: more inventory, more staff, more logistics, more moving parts. Every extra dollar of revenue tends to bring a matching dose of stress. It's like running on a treadmill that speeds up with every step.

That's the trap a lot of entrepreneurs fall into. Growth looks exciting from the outside, but inside, it feels like you're sprinting just to stay in place.

But digital businesses play by a different set of rules. They scale without scaling your stress.

Say you've got a blog or a newsletter. If your audience grows from 1,000 to 10,000 readers a day, your workload doesn't go up tenfold. Maybe your hosting bill bumps up a few bucks, but the system still runs while you sleep.

Or take something simple, like an ebook or a course. You write it once. And whether 10 people buy it or 10,000, the product doesn't ask for more of your time. It just delivers. Quietly, efficiently, and automatically.

That's real leverage. With digital assets, you can grow earnings without growing effort. You can make more without doing more.

It's a bit like owning a toll booth on a digital highway. Once it's built, every extra car that drives through just means more money in your pocket, without adding a single minute to your workday.

That's not just magic. That's smart business.

You Can Be the Owner, Not Just a Shareholder

"We are comfortable both with total ownership of businesses and with marketable securities representing small portions of businesses." — 1981 Berkshire Hathaway Shareholder Letter

When you buy a stock, you're a fractional owner of a big machine you don't control. You're tagging along, hoping the CEO makes the right decisions and that Wall Street doesn't panic the next time there's a headline.

But when you buy a small online business, you're not along for the ride. You're in the driver's seat.

It's all yours. You control the product. You choose what to optimize or outsource. And best of all, you're not watching stock tickers or quarterly earnings calls. You're thinking long term, because now you actually have that control.

In theory, liquidity in the stock market is a good thing. You can buy or sell with the click of a button. But in practice? That convenience becomes a trap for a lot of investors. When markets drop, emotions kick in, and people sell at exactly the wrong time.

With a private business, it's different. You're not watching price charts or reacting to headlines. You're focused on the business itself, the operations, the growth, the cash flow. Ownership forces you to think long term. You stop acting like a trader and start thinking like a builder. And that shift in mindset might be one of the biggest advantages of all.

And here's the twist: these businesses aren't just affordable; they're shockingly affordable. You can get started for as little as a few thousand dollars. That's the kind of ownership Buffett talks about, just scaled to our size.

The Power of Cheap Capital

In one of his classic shareholder letters, Buffett wrote, "Our cost of funds has been less than nothing." He was talking about float, the money insurance companies collect now but don't have to pay out until later. That "free" capital became one of the biggest engines behind Berkshire's long-term success.

Now, most of us don't own insurance companies. But in the world of online business acquisitions, you can create your own version of float, if you know how to structure the deal.

Many times, sellers are open to financing part of the sale themselves, which means you're essentially buying the business with their money. Other times, you can arrange an earn-out, where a portion of the price is paid only if the business performs well after the handoff. And if the deal is the right size, you may qualify for low-interest small business loans that reduce the upfront cash needed.

I've seen and negotiated deals where I only had to put up a small fraction of the purchase price out of pocket. When the business is solid and cash-flowing from day one, that kind of leverage can dramatically boost your return.

Why would the seller ever want to do that? From a buyer's perspective, this is a no-brainer. You reduce your upfront capital, lower your risk, and start generating cash flow before you've even finished paying for the business.

But here's the part most first-time buyers overlook: seller financing is actually a win for the seller too, especially when you understand the tax implications.

If a seller receives the full purchase price upfront, they typically owe capital gains taxes on the entire amount that year. That can create a hefty tax bill, especially if the sale pushes them into a higher bracket.

But if the deal is structured as installment payments over time, the seller only owes taxes on what they receive each year. That can soften the tax blow and help them spread out their gains, sometimes allowing them to keep more of the proceeds in the long run.

And here's the other piece: for many sellers, especially solo operators, a lump sum of cash can feel overwhelming. A steady stream of income over a few years, almost like a paycheck, might actually fit their financial goals better.

So when you propose seller financing, you're not just asking for a favor. You're offering a flexible, tax-friendly option that benefits them too.

Why Flexibility Is Your Secret Weapon

"I feel substantially greater size is more likely to harm future results than to help them." — 2016 Berkshire Hathaway Shareholder Letter

In one of his later shareholder letters, Buffett admitted something you don't hear often from billionaires: managing a huge portfolio can actually be a disadvantage. When you're sitting on $100 billion, it's tough to find investments that move the needle. The pool of available opportunities shrinks, not because there are fewer great businesses, but because most of them are too small to matter at that scale.

We don't have that problem.

As individual investors, we can go anywhere. Public stocks, small private deals, content sites, KDP portfolios—you name it. That kind of flexibility is a real edge. It gives us more opportunities to find businesses that are mis-priced, overlooked, or underperforming for reasons we know how to fix.

I still scan the public markets regularly. But more and more, I find better value, and better returns, on the private side. The deals are smaller, sure. But so is the competition. And when you're investing your own capital, that freedom to look wherever the value is? It's one of the most powerful advantages you have.

Let's Be Honest, This Isn't a Free Lunch

Before we go any further, I want to be clear: there's no magic here. No secret formula. You will not stumble into wealth by clicking a few buttons.

Buying and owning an online business isn't like buying a stock. Stocks let you sit back while someone else runs the company. In this world, you are the one in charge, which means there's real work involved.

Learn First, Then Earn

Before you can own a business the right way, whether it's a content site, a digital product, or something else entirely, you've got to understand how the model actually works.

Where does the money come from? What drives traffic? What levers can you pull to improve results? These aren't just academic questions. They're the keys to making good decisions once you're in the owner's seat.

That's exactly why this book exists: to walk you through the nuts and bolts so you're not flying blind.

Now, here's the encouraging part: once you've done the learning and built the right systems, a lot of the day-to-day can run without you. I've had businesses that were 90% hands-off. Customer emails got answered, content got updated, and revenue kept coming in even while I was on vacation with my kid. But I didn't start there.

To get to that point, you've got to do the work upfront. You need to build competence. Buffett didn't wake up knowing how to analyze a company. He sat down, read thousands of pages, and trained himself to think like an owner. That early effort became his edge.

It's the same here. No, it's not passive in the beginning. You're laying the foundation. You're figuring things out. But every hour you invest now becomes a source of leverage later. The business starts returning your time back to you with interest.

It's Not Set-It-and-Forget-It, and That's Okay

Let's be real for a second. Online businesses, especially things like content sites or Kindle book portfolios, can run with surprisingly little day-to-day involvement once they're humming along. That's one reason they're so attractive.

But let's not kid ourselves. They don't run on autopilot.

Every now and then, something needs your attention. A blog post falls out of date. A freelancer turns in work that doesn't quite hit the mark. Your website isn't working because of a problem with one of its add-ons. Or maybe your Amazon royalties dip, and you need to figure out why.

It's not chaos. It's just business ownership. Even Buffett checks in on his portfolio from time to time.

But here's the good news: you don't have to do it all yourself. With a little upfront effort and the right systems in place, you can outsource most of the routine stuff. Updating content, posting to social media, managing customer emails — it's all stuff you can delegate once you've built the playbook.

The goal here isn't hands-off. That's a fantasy. The goal is hands-light, where you're steering the ship, but you're not rowing every oar.

That's still a fantastic deal. You get the control and cash flow of owning a real business, with a fraction of the grind that usually comes with it. It's not passive income, but it's leveraged, flexible, and miles ahead of trading time for money.

Due Diligence Is Everything

Here's the truth no one likes to hear: buying the wrong business can cost you far more than just money. It can drain your time, your energy, and, maybe worst of all, your confidence.

That's why due diligence isn't just a box to check. It's the difference between a smart deal and an expensive lesson.

When you're doing due diligence, you're not taking the seller's word for it. You're verifying the numbers. You're checking where the traffic actually comes from. You're asking, "Is this income repeatable?" and "What's likely to break if I take this over?" You're looking for cracks before they become sinkholes.

The good news? You don't need to be a CPA or an SEO ninja to get this right. You just need a clear process and a bit of discipline, the same way Buffett reviews a business before buying in. He doesn't need to swing at every pitch. He waits for the fat one right over the plate.

That's what I'll show you in this book: how to do simple, effective due diligence that protects your downside and builds your confidence. After a few reps, your instincts get sharper. You'll start spotting what matters and what's just noise in less than 30 minutes.

You're Not the Only One Hunting for Deals

Some years ago, buying online businesses felt like discovering a secret fishing hole. Hardly anyone was casting a line, and if you knew what you were doing, you could reel in a solid catch without much competition.

But things are changing.

More people are waking up to the opportunity. More capital is pouring into the space. And naturally, the competition is starting to heat up. It's still nothing like the public markets, not even close. But the days of stumbling into a great deal without effort are fading.

That doesn't mean you should sit it out. It just means you've got to sharpen your game.

Buffett said it best: "A truly great business must have an enduring moat." That moat, whether it's loyal customers, dominant SEO rankings, strong brand recognition, or a niche that's hard to crack, is what protects a business when competition shows up.

And the good news? Those moats still exist in online business. Lots of them. The market may be growing, but it's still full of inefficiencies. The trick is knowing what to look for and how to separate a business riding a temporary wave from one that's built to last.

In the chapters ahead, we'll break that down together. Because if you want to win in a more crowded field, you don't need to be the fastest or flashiest. You just need to be the most prepared.

Final Word

No investment comes without risk. Anyone who tells you otherwise is either lying or selling something.

But here's the truth most people miss: some games offer better odds than others. And online business, when approached with care and common sense, is one of those games.

You're entering a space with more flexibility, fewer gatekeepers, and far less competition than the public markets. There's no army of analysts picking over every deal. No hedge funds bidding up prices before you even get a look. And best of all, you're not just along for the ride; you're in the driver's seat.

That control, the ability to influence the outcome, is something you rarely get as a stockholder. In this world, your effort and judgment matter. You can make the business better. You can steer the strategy. You can choose how the story plays out.

Even more encouraging? This is a space where Buffett's principles still work, and they're not yet played out. Margin of safety.

Moats. Intrinsic value. Most buyers in this market don't even speak that language, which means if you do, you're already ahead.

The rest of this book will walk you through the full playbook: how to evaluate an online business, negotiate a fair deal, and grow what you've bought into something meaningful. You don't need to be a genius. But you do need to think like an owner.

And if you can do that patiently, rationally, and with a little curiosity, you'll be surprised at what's possible.

Chapter Two

Think Like Buffett: The Investor Mindset for the Digital Age

This Isn't a Get-Rich-Quick Play, and That's a Good Thing

L ET ME BE STRAIGHT with you. If you picked up this book hoping for a secret blueprint to flip $500 into $50,000 by next month, you're going to be disappointed. That's not what this is.

This isn't a "one weird trick" kind of story. There are no overnight windfalls here. No magic funnels. No plug-and-play passive income hacks.

What we're talking about is real investing, the kind Buffett and Munger would recognize. You're buying real businesses. They make real money. They serve real people. And they take real work to understand and operate.

Can it be profitable? Absolutely. I've seen deals that paid for themselves in under two years. Businesses bought for five figures that quietly spit out steady income month after month. I've seen others double or triple in value after a few smart improvements. Some even grew into full-time careers or sold for life-changing exits.

But none of those results came from chasing shortcuts. They came from treating online business like business, not like a lottery ticket.

It's no different from buying a small brick-and-mortar company, except the overhead is lower and the leverage is better. You're not just tossing money into a black box and hoping for the best. You're stepping into the role of owner. That means asking hard questions, analyzing the fundamentals, and thinking beyond the next 30 days.

And yes, that means making some mistakes too. That's part of the process. You'll misread a traffic pattern. Hire the wrong freelancer. Miss a red flag that was there in plain sight. It happens. But you learn, you adjust, and you get better.

The beauty of this space is that the learning curve is steep at first, but it flattens quickly. With each deal, your instincts sharpen. Your playbook gets tighter. And suddenly, what once felt overwhelming starts to feel like second nature.

The hardest part is ignoring the noise.

Ignore the YouTube ads promising "set it and forget it" income with zero effort. Ignore the hype around trending niches that burn out faster than a TikTok dance. And please, never take a seller's word when they say, "This business practically runs itself."

Ask questions. Dig into the numbers. Stay skeptical, but curious.

You don't need to swing for the fences on your first deal. You just need to get in the game and stay in it long enough to let compounding, in both knowledge and returns, do its job.

Buffett once said, "The stock market is designed to transfer money from the impatient to the patient." He could've just as easily been talking about online business.

Because, in the end, patience beats hustle. Diligence beats hype. And a well-bought, well-run digital business will beat chasing the next shiny object almost every time.

It's not fast. But it's real. And that's what makes it work.

Don't Fall in Love With the Deal

This is one of the oldest traps in the book. I've seen plenty of investors fall into it. I've stepped right into it myself.

It usually starts the same way. You come across a business that looks promising. The numbers check out. The revenue is steady. You start picturing the upside: the passive income, the flexibility, maybe even quitting your job someday.

And just like that, you're emotionally attached.

You haven't bought the business yet, but in your mind, you already own it. You've named the upside. You've made it personal. And that's when the blind spots creep in.

You overlook little red flags. You rationalize obvious flaws. You tell yourself, "That traffic dip is seasonal." Or "Sure, the content's outdated, but I can fix that easily." You ease up in negotiations. You stretch your budget. Worst of all, you stop asking the tough questions because you want it to work out.

I get it. It's human nature. But it's also how smart investors end up with bad businesses.

Buffett has a rule: "The most important thing to do if you find yourself in a hole is to stop digging." That applies here, too. The best investors I know treat every deal like just one of many, not their one shot at success. They stay emotionally detached. Curious, yes. Hopeful, maybe. But not attached.

They know there's always another deal around the corner. And they understand that the real cost of falling in love too early isn't just money; it's time, energy, and opportunity cost.

When you let emotions lead, you lose your edge. But when you stay grounded, when you can walk away from a deal without regret, you protect your downside and preserve your ability to act when the right opportunity shows up.

So don't chase a deal just because you want it to work. Stick to your principles. Ask the hard questions. And if something doesn't add up, be willing to say no, even if you've already started dreaming about what life would look like post-acquisition.

Trust me: your best deal is still out there. And you'll be far more prepared to recognize it when you're not tangled up in the wrong one.

Wait for the Fat Pitch

Warren Buffett once said, "The stock market is a no-called-strike game. You don't have to swing at everything. You can wait for your pitch."

That idea has stuck with me for years. It's simple, but powerful, especially for buying online businesses.

In this world, no one's forcing your hand. There's no shot clock. You don't have to buy the first deal that looks interesting. Or the fifth. Or even the fiftieth. Your job, in the beginning, isn't to act; it's to observe.

Watch the market. Study the listings. Ask questions. Get a feel for what makes a business valuable and, just as importantly, what should make you walk away.

I usually recommend giving yourself a few months to look around before making a move. Run the numbers. Talk to sellers. Compare deals. The more reps you get, the faster your instincts sharpen. Eventually, you'll come across a listing that just clicks. The numbers make sense. The story holds up. You've seen enough now to say, "That's the one."

And if you really want to level up your understanding, try building something from scratch. A blog, a small content site, maybe even a couple of Kindle books. It won't make you rich overnight, but it'll teach you what goes into creating value. You'll see how hard it is to get traffic. How long it takes to rank on Google. How much effort goes into just earning that first dollar.

And when you've lived that, even a little, you'll have a whole new appreciation for the power of buying something that's already working.

Here's the thing: the best deals don't usually go to the fastest bidder. They go to the most prepared. The one who's studied the game, waited patiently, and is ready to swing hard when the fat pitch finally comes down the middle.

So don't rush it. Don't force it. This isn't about being first; it's about being right.

The best deals come to those who are patient and prepared to swing when it counts.

You'll Make Mistakes, And That's Part of the Process

Let's be honest right out of the gate: you're going to screw something up.

You'll misread a trend. Overpay for a business that looked better on paper than it performed in real life. Hire the wrong freelancer. Miss a red flag in the financials that was staring you in the face. It's not a matter of if; it's a matter of when.

And that's okay.

It's not a sign that you're failing. It's a sign that you're learning. Every experienced investor, whether they're buying stocks, real estate, or digital businesses, has a story or two (or twenty) about a deal that didn't go quite as planned.

The key isn't to avoid all mistakes. That's impossible. The key is to keep your mistakes small. Manageable. Contained. That's how you stay in the game long enough to get better.

This is why I always tell first-time buyers: don't try to hit a home run on your first deal. Don't risk more than you can afford, financially or emotionally. Treat that first purchase as tuition. You're paying to learn, just like Buffett did when he bought Cities Service

Preferred at age 11. He sold too early, missed the bigger gain, and learned a priceless lesson about patience.

What matters most is what you do after the mistake.

Do you get discouraged and quit? Or do you pause, reflect, and adjust? The best investors I know don't get rattled by a loss. They get curious. They go back and ask, "Where did my thinking go wrong?" Then they course-correct. They take the lesson. And they move on, a little smarter, a little sharper, and far more dangerous the next time around.

And remember this: in investing, survival is underrated. If you can avoid blowing yourself up early, the compounding of capital and knowledge takes over.

So yes, you'll make mistakes. Everyone does. But if you manage your downside, stay humble, and treat every deal as a chance to learn, you'll come out ahead in the long run.

Start Small or Go Big? It Depends on You

One of the most common questions people ask when they first step into the world of online business investing is, "How big should my first deal be?"

And the honest answer is: it depends. There's no perfect number. No universal starting point. And anyone who insists otherwise probably hasn't done this for real.

That said, if you're looking for my advice, I suggest you start small.

Buying a smaller deal, something in the $1,000 to $5,000 range, gives you the chance to learn without risking too much. You'll get to experience the entire process firsthand: evaluating a deal, asking the right questions, managing the transition, and operating the business post-acquisition. And trust me, even a small content site or digital product can teach you a lot. I've built a few sites from scratch myself over the years, mostly as weekend projects. They weren't big earners, but they were excellent teachers.

There's something valuable about getting your hands dirty. When it's your money on the line, even just a few thousand dollars, you start paying attention to the right things: traffic quality, monetization methods, conversion rates, content quality. And most importantly, you start building your own judgment, which no book or course can hand you.

That said, I've also seen people succeed by starting big right out of the gate. They come in with $50,000 or $100,000 to deploy, and they buy more established businesses with stronger systems, cleaner financials, and more stable revenue. If someone has the capital, relevant experience, and a clear goal, such as replacing a job or building a portfolio quickly, that approach can absolutely work.

But here's the thing: buying big doesn't guarantee smooth sailing. Bigger deals come with bigger complexity and bigger risks if you miss something. If you don't have the reps yet, you may not know what to look for, what questions to ask, or how to spot the red flags hiding in plain sight.

So if you're starting from scratch, I believe the smart move is to start small. Learn how this world works. Make your early mistakes where they're affordable. Build your confidence and skill set slowly. And when you're ready to go bigger, you'll do it with far more clarity and control.

There's no rush. There's no right or wrong answer here. Just match the deal size to your budget, your goals, and your comfort level. The important thing is that you start and learn in a way that sets you up for the long game.

Begin with the Exit in Mind

Buffett once said, "Our favorite holding period is forever." And in a perfect world, that's how we'd all invest, buying great businesses and holding them indefinitely. But life doesn't always work that way.

At some point, you might want or need to sell.

Maybe growth has leveled off, and it's time to lock in gains. Maybe you're no longer interested in running the business day-to-day. Or maybe a new opportunity comes along and you need the capital. Whatever the reason, planning for an exit isn't a sign of short-term thinking. It's a sign you're building with intention.

That's what long-term owners do. They build something that's not just profitable, but transferable.

So how do you do that?

Start by separating the business from your personal identity. This is one reason I usually steer clear of YouTube channels. They're often built around the creator's face or personality, which makes them tough to transfer. The more your business stands on its own, the easier it is to sell.

Next, document your systems. Create clear, step-by-step instructions for how things run, from publishing new content to managing freelancers to tracking revenue. Think of it like building a user manual for your future buyer. Standard operating procedures [SOP] don't just help you; they raise the value of the business.

And finally, keep your books clean. Use accounting software or hire a part-time bookkeeper to stay on top of your financials. When the time comes to sell, this will save you hours of stress and make your business far more attractive to serious buyers.

The truth is, the easier your business is to understand, run, and scale, the more valuable it becomes. And even if you never sell, building with that mindset gives you more clarity, more control, and a stronger asset in the long run.

Treat Each Deal Like a Real Business

In the beginning, it's totally fine, even smart, to treat your first acquisition like an experiment. You're learning how deals work. You're getting a feel for digital revenue models, maybe managing content or contractors for the first time. You're dipping your toes in the water without diving all the way in. And honestly, that early trial-and-error stage is where some of the most valuable learning happens.

But if your goal is to grow, to turn this into something meaningful, then at some point, you have to make the mental shift from hobbyist to business owner.

That shift changes everything.

You stop thinking in terms of "a website" or "a KDP account" and start thinking in terms of systems, margins, customer experience, and durability. You realize you're not just acquiring digital assets. You're buying businesses with real customers, cash flow, and risk. And that requires a different level of thinking.

You start asking better questions:What's the cost to acquire a customer?What does retention look like?How defensible is this business, and what's stopping someone from copying it tomorrow?What's the moat, and is it getting wider or thinner?

That mindset shift also shows up in how you handle operations. Eventually, you'll want to separate your business finances from your personal ones. In my case, I formed an LLC in my home state from the start. It was simpler than I expected. I watched a few YouTube tutorials, filed the paperwork online, and opened a business bank account and credit card a couple of weeks later.

Was it overkill for a business making a few hundred dollars a month at the beginning of my journey? Maybe. But what it did was signal to myself that I was building something serious. Something I could grow, track, and eventually sell.

Now, I'm not a lawyer or CPA, so take this as personal experience, not professional advice. You'll want to do your own research and choose the legal and tax structure that fits your situation.

The point isn't to make things complicated. In fact, the simpler and more organized you keep things, the easier it is to scale later.

The key is this: treat each deal, even the small ones, like a real business. Because that's exactly what they are. And the more seriously you take them, the more seriously they'll reward you.

This isn't just about income. It's about building something durable. Something that grows with you. Something that, one day, someone else might want to buy. Not because of the cash flow alone, but because of how well you built the foundation.

Final Word

Take your time. There's no race here. No leaderboard, no buzzer going off, and no one handing out medals for how fast you buy your first business.

This isn't about speed. It's about staying power.

Too many people rush into their first deal because they feel like they're falling behind. They see a success story online or hear someone talk about a big flip and think, "I need to catch up." But wealth built in a hurry usually disappears in a hurry, too. What actually works, what always works, is steady, thoughtful progress over time.

You don't need to get it all right the first time. You just need to bring the right mindset to the table. If you lead with curiosity, patience, and a willingness to learn, you'll avoid most of the big, painful mistakes. And more importantly, you'll start developing the skills that compound.

This game isn't about chasing shortcuts. It's not about building something flashy, brag-worthy, or built on hype. It's about buying real digital assets, ones with real cash flow and staying power. And doing it with discipline. With a clear head. With the same kind of long-term thinking Buffett has preached for decades.

You're not just collecting websites or side hustles. You're building a portfolio. One piece at a time. Thoughtfully. Intentionally.

That shift, from opportunist to owner, from dabbling to investing, is where everything changes. Because once you start thinking like a true investor, you stop chasing quick wins and start planting seeds. And those seeds, if you nurture them, will grow into something meaningful.

So take your time. Play your game. And build something that lasts.

Chapter Three

Moats on the Web: How to Spot Online Businesses Built to Last

"WHAT WE'RE TRYING TO do is we're trying to find a business with a wide and long-lasting moat around it, protecting a terrific economic castle with an honest lord in charge of the castle." — Warren Buffett at the 1995 Berkshire Hathaway

Just like the stock market is made up of different industries, such as tech, healthcare, and consumer goods, the world of online businesses also breaks down into distinct models. And each one comes with its own set of trade-offs.

Some models are hands-on and fast-moving. Others are slower-paced and more passive. Some require technical know-how or customer service skills. Others can run quietly in the background with the right systems in place.

The key is knowing which model fits you: your goals, your time, and your skillset. Because the better the fit, the more likely you'll find a business you can run well and grow confidently.

In this next section, we'll break down the most common online business models, how they work, and how to spot a moat — that built-in advantage that keeps competition at bay. Understanding these differences isn't just academic. It's how you'll filter deals, focus your search, and invest with clarity. Let's get into it.

Beginner-friendly Models with Natural Moats

The Upside of Content Sites (When Done Right)

In Buffett's early days, few businesses were as attractive as a dominant local newspaper. In his 1984 Berkshire Hathaway letter, he put it plainly:

"The economics of a dominant newspaper are excellent, among the very best in the business world. Once dominant, the newspaper itself, not the marketplace, determines just how good or how bad the paper will be. Good or bad, it will prosper."

That same dynamic — high-margin, low-capital, defensible — still exists today. But now, you're more likely to find it in a well-run content site.

A content site is essentially a digital newspaper for a niche audience. Instead of printing on paper, you publish online. The product isn't a physical good or even software. It's the content itself. Articles, guides, videos, reviews... anything useful, entertaining, or educational that draws in readers.

These sites generate revenue in a few simple ways: display ads, affiliate links, sponsored content, digital products, or subscriptions. If the site ranks well in search engines or builds a loyal following, it becomes a kind of mini-media asset, one that throws off steady cash flow with very little ongoing capital required.

And just like newspapers of old, dominance matters. A content site that owns its niche, whether it's gardening tips, tech tutorials, or hiking gear reviews, gets to control the game. It becomes the go-to source. It earns trust, attention, and revenue, often quietly, and often for years.

Not every content site wins, of course. But when you find (or build) one with a loyal audience, stable traffic, and defensible rankings, the economics can be excellent.

Buffett loved newspapers because once they held the top spot, the economics followed. In today's world, content sites offer a modern version of that same opportunity: they're lean, scalable, and quietly powerful.

For example, think about something like Healthline. If you Google "symptoms of vitamin D deficiency," you'll probably land on one of their articles. They're not selling you a pill directly. But their content brings in millions of readers a month, and that traffic earns them money through advertising and product referrals. That's a content site.

Or take NerdWallet. It started as a basic blog comparing credit cards. Over time, it grew into a full-blown content business with deep guides on mortgages, investing, and insurance. They don't sell financial products. They educate you on your options, then earn a commission if you sign up through their links. That's affiliate marketing. NerdWallet is now a public company worth $600M as of this writing. But at its core, it's just a very smart content site.

Even niche examples work. A friend of mine once bought a small website that published reviews of espresso machines. It got around 30,000 visits a month and made money through Amazon affiliate links. Every time someone clicked through and bought a $500 machine, he got a cut. The site didn't invent anything new. It just ranked well on Google and answered people's questions better than the competition.

So, in simple terms: content sites are digital real estate. The content is what brings people through the front door, and once they're inside, you find a way to monetize that attention.

The beauty of a content site is that it can scale without much extra fuel. Once you've built a strong SEO foundation and have a clear niche, growth is often just a matter of publishing more high-quality content. You don't need warehouses or a sales team; just smart strategy and consistent execution. And when you find untapped keywords or content gaps, you can expand with minimal extra cost.

And here's where it really gets interesting: once a piece of content ranks on Google, it can earn passively for months or even years. It's not quite "set it and forget it," but it's pretty close. One solid article can become a digital asset, pulling in traffic and generating income 24/7. It's like buying a rental unit that keeps paying rent while you sleep.

Warren Buffett once said, "If you don't find a way to make money while you sleep, you will work until you die." Content sites are a great example of that.

What's more, that traffic is free. Unlike an e-commerce store that has to keep paying for ads, SEO-driven content doesn't cost anything once it's live and ranking. And because you're not shipping products or dealing with returns, your overhead stays low. No inventory. No customer support. Often just a couple of freelancers and a good hosting setup.

The margins reflect that. After your upfront investment in content creation, many sites can run at 70%–90% profit margins, especially if you're not in hyper-growth mode. That kind of efficiency is hard to beat.

Revenue also isn't tied to one stream. The best sites make money in a few different ways: display ads from networks like Mediavine or AdThrive, affiliate links (Amazon or niche programs), sponsored posts, downloadable products, or even building a subscriber base you can market to directly.

Now, let's talk about *Moats* — what makes a good site defensible.

The strongest sites dominate their niche. They rank for thousands of keywords, have real authority in Google's eyes, and own the conversation in their corner of the internet, whether it's home espresso machines, minimalist travel, or DIY woodworking.

These sites usually have a deep content library, not just fluff. Well-structured, well-researched content with internal links, expert quotes, and helpful formatting. That's tough and expensive to replicate. It's not just content; it's an asset.

The cherry on top? A real audience. If a site has brand recognition, loyal readers, an email list, or even a social following, you've got something that can't be easily copied. That direct traffic is gold. It's less fragile than SEO, and it means people choose to come back to you.

The Risks (And Why Not All Content Sites Are Created Equal)

Let's not sugarcoat it, content sites aren't all upside. Like any investment, they come with risks. Some are obvious. Others are sneaky. All of them are worth understanding before you write the check.

The biggest wildcard? Google.

If your traffic depends on search, then Google holds the keys to the castle. One algorithm update — with no warning, no rollback, and no human to explain it — can knock your rankings off a cliff overnight. You could go to bed with a profitable site and wake up to a 50% drop in traffic and income. That's not theoretical; it happens all the time.

That's why diversification matters, both in traffic and in revenue. If your entire site is riding on one article, one affiliate product, or one ad partner, you're walking a tightrope without a net. I've seen sites making $5,000 a month from one well-placed Amazon link. Until Amazon cut affiliate commissions, and just like that, it dropped to $1,000. No warning. No negotiation. Just a new policy.

And then there's the issue of aging content. Even "evergreen" posts need upkeep. Google wants fresh, accurate, relevant content, not stale listicles from 2019. If the previous owner neglected updates, or worse, filled the site with thin, keyword-stuffed posts, you could be inheriting a liability disguised as an asset.

There's also a darker side of SEO: the shortcut crowd. Some sellers juice their traffic with shady link-building schemes, expired domain tricks, or AI-generated fluff dressed up as real content. It might look good on the surface. Traffic is up, revenue is solid, but it's built on sand. When Google catches on (and it always does), those rankings vanish, and you're left holding the bag.

And let's not forget the structural risk: no brand, no audience, no moat. If the site doesn't have a loyal following, an email list, or a clear voice, then it's just a collection of words on a screen. Easy to copy. Easy to compete with. If someone can replicate your top pages with a better design or faster site speed, they can siphon off your traffic in months.

Here's the takeaway: a great content site is like owning a small, profitable media company. It may not be flashy, but if it has a solid SEO foundation, a clear niche, an engaged audience, and diversified income streams, it can throw off stable cash flow with excellent margins. That's the kind of business Buffett would appreciate. Steady, boring, durable.

But not every site is what it seems. Some look like castles, but they're really just houses of cards propped up by short-term hacks and risky assumptions.

So do your homework. Ask hard questions. Understand the risks, not just the revenue. Because in this space, buying the wrong content site isn't just a bad investment. It's a lesson you pay for in both time and money.

And the better you get at spotting what's real, the easier it becomes to buy with confidence and build something that lasts.

The AI Risk: What's Still Defensible in a World Full of Content?

If you're investing in content sites, whether you're building them yourself or buying them, you can't ignore the elephant in the room: AI (Artificial Intelligence). It's changing the game fast, and depending on how your site is positioned, it's either a headwind or a hurricane.

I've been investing in online content businesses for years now. And if there's one rule that's held up, it's this: you make money by owning attention, not just publishing content. But the gap between those two has never been more important than it is today, and AI is widening that gap.

Because here's the hard truth: content creation is no longer scarce. With tools like ChatGPT, Jasper, and dozens more AI copywriters popping up, almost anyone can generate thousands of words in minutes. And a lot of them are. That means the sheer volume of content on the internet is exploding. But attention? That's still scarce.

So the question every investor should ask before buying or scaling a content site now is: what happens when the internet is flooded with average content?

And more importantly: what makes this site defensible in a world where anyone can spin up 10 blog posts before breakfast?

Let's start with the risk.

AI is exceptionally good at producing surface-level content. Basic how-tos, listicles, summaries... anything with a clear structure and publicly available information is now easier, cheaper, and faster to create than ever before. That means content sites built purely on SEO and commodity information are in real trouble. I'm talking about sites that rely on affiliate roundups, shallow reviews, "best of" lists, or generic tips in popular niches. A lot of them were already walking a tightrope. AI just cut the safety net.

If your content can be written by a robot, and still satisfy the average user, then you're playing a dangerous game. Search engines are already flooded with copycat content. And while Google still talks a good game about prioritizing "experience" and "originality," the results tell a murkier story. Even if AI-generated pages get filtered out eventually, you're still competing with an ocean of cheap content. The cost of standing out just went up.

From an investor's perspective, that changes how I evaluate sites.

When I look at a deal now, I'm not just asking how much content it has or how well it ranks. I'm asking: What's unique here? What's personal? What's hard to replicate?

And that's where you start to see a clear divide between vulnerable and resilient content businesses.

Vulnerable content sites tend to follow a familiar pattern. They're built around high-volume keywords, optimized for ads or affiliate clicks, and rely on content that doesn't require expertise or perspective. Think general advice blogs, broad lifestyle content, shallow product reviews, or recipe sites with no real story behind the food. These sites are easy to spin up, easy to scale... and easy to replace.

Defensible content sites, the kind that still make sense to build or buy in an AI-saturated world, are built on more than just keywords and clever formatting. They're grounded in trust, real-world experience, and a level of specificity that's hard to fake, especially for a machine.

What makes these sites stand out is that the content doesn't just exist; it belongs to someone. It reflects lived experience. You can tell when you're reading something written by a person who's been there. A parent writing about raising a child with ADHD, for example, speaks from a place no generic content generator can reach. You feel the difference. It's not just information; it's insight. And that gives the content weight.

These sites also have a distinct voice. Not just in tone or style, but in perspective. There's a worldview behind the writing, a sense that you're hearing from someone, not just reading another article. That sense of voice, whether it's witty, blunt, warm, or sharp, builds loyalty. People don't just come back for the advice. They come back because they trust the person giving it. And in a noisy world filled with sameness, the voice becomes a moat.

Just as important, the strongest content businesses don't rely entirely on Google to bring people in. They've built direct relationships, through email, products, or a loyal reader base that seeks them out. That kind of connection insulates them from algorithm shifts. It gives them leverage. Because when people opt into your list, buy your book, or visit your site regularly by choice, you're not just capturing traffic. You're building equity.

These are the kinds of sites that still have long-term value. Not because they're the biggest. But because they're real, defensible, and rooted in something AI still can't replicate: human trust.

That's what I have been thinking lately as an investor. Content businesses that are slow to build but hard to copy.

In fact, I'd argue that quality content sites are about to get more valuable, not less. Because as the internet becomes noisier and more robotic, the demand for human, trustworthy, credible content actually goes up. Readers are going to be hungry for signal in a world full of AI noise. They won't trust the first result. They'll want proof. Voice. Realness. Context.

And that's where the opportunity lies.

AI won't kill content businesses. But it will expose them. It'll force creators and investors to ask deeper questions: Why does this content matter? Who is it for? And what gives it the right to exist?

If the answers are clear, compelling, and rooted in something real, that site still has a future. Maybe even a brighter one.

But if the answers are vague, if the content could be generated by a machine and no one would know the difference, then you're holding a melting ice cube.

So if you're in this space — building, buying, or scaling — now's the time to get honest about the business you're in. You're not just publishing content anymore. You're building a connection. And connection can't be outsourced.

Not to AI.Not at scale.Not yet, and maybe not ever.

Amazon KDP

Imagine you've got a story to tell. Or maybe you've spent years learning something, a skill, a subject, a unique perspective, that could help other people. In the past, the only way to share that knowledge in book form was to chase down a traditional publisher, pitch your manuscript, and hope someone gave you a shot.

But that gatekeeping era is over.

Thanks to Amazon Kindle Direct Publishing (KDP), anyone with an idea and a bit of follow-through can turn their words into a real, published book. One that's instantly available to millions of readers across the globe.

Turning Books Into Passive Income Streams

Amazon KDP is one of the most overlooked ways everyday people are building digital assets that quietly generate income.

Think of it like owning a bookstore that's open 24/7, serving customers in every time zone, but without the headaches of inventory, printing, or shipping. No staff. No overhead. No landlord breathing down your neck. Just a handful of well-written books sitting on Amazon's virtual shelves, earning royalties around the clock.

Whether you're publishing books, you wrote yourself or acquiring a portfolio of titles someone else created, KDP is a self-serve publishing machine. You upload the manuscript, choose your price, and Amazon takes it from there. Digital distribution, paperback printing, payment processing, and even customer service. It's publishing with a backend built for scale.

Here's why it gets interesting from an investor's perspective: once a book is live, properly formatted, and ranked, it can produce income with almost no day-to-day effort. No customer emails. No order fulfillment. No inventory to manage. It's one of the purest forms of leverage out there. You do the work once, and it keeps working for you.

Sure, not every book is a bestseller. But when done right, with quality content, smart keywords, and clear market demand, a single title can turn into a steady stream of royalties. A whole catalog? That's a digital portfolio with real cash flow potential.

It's not flashy. It's not overnight. But it's real. And for anyone looking to own income-producing assets without the complexity of physical operations, KDP is a surprisingly powerful way to do just that.

You're not just writing books. You're building a system and turning ideas into income.

The Print-on-Demand Model: Low Risk, High Leverage

One of the most underrated advantages of Amazon KDP is its print-on-demand model. And for investors, it's one of the most powerful levers in the entire ecosystem.

Here's how it works: you don't print anything upfront. You don't bulk order 1,000 copies and hope they sell. You don't store boxes in your garage or pay for warehouse space to house unsold inventory. In fact, you never touch the product at all.

Instead, Amazon only prints a paperback copy of your book after a customer places an order. That single shift changes the economics completely.

Because now, your overhead is almost nonexistent. There's no cash tied up in inventory. No risk of overestimating demand and sitting on unsold stock. You create the content once, upload the file, and Amazon handles everything else: printing, packing, shipping, and even dealing with customer service issues.

That means your capital isn't trapped in physical products. It's freed up to invest in new titles, ads, or other assets. You can scale your publishing portfolio without the traditional burdens of a product-based business.

And your margins stay clean. Yes, Amazon takes its cut, but you don't have to deal with manufacturing costs, fulfillment centers, or returns logistics. You're earning royalties from a product that technically doesn't even exist until someone buys it. That's the beauty of digital-physical hybrid models: they give you the reach and legitimacy of a physical book, with the cash flow and scalability of a digital business.

For investors, this is gold. Because now you're not just betting on a book. You're betting on a model that minimizes downside while leaving the upside wide open. You don't need a team, a warehouse, or a shipping label. You just need content people want to read.

And once it's live, every sale is a small but steady return on the asset you built, without lifting another finger.

The Royalty Model: Get Paid While You Sleep

And then there's the royalty model, the engine that turns your content into income.

Every time someone buys your book on Amazon, you earn a royalty. Depending on the price you set and the region where the book is sold, that royalty is typically either 35% or 70% of the sale price for eBooks. For print books, it's generally 60% minus printing cost. Not a onetime fee, not a flat payout, but a recurring slice of revenue for every copy sold, no matter where or when it happens.

That means if someone in New York downloads your ebook at 3 p.m., or a reader in Tokyo buys your paperback at 3 a.m., you're getting paid. Automatically. You don't have to ship a thing, answer a question, or even be awake.

It's one of the purest forms of digital income out there and one of the most appealing parts of the KDP platform for investors.

Unlike traditional businesses where you trade time for money, the royalty model flips the script. You front-load the effort: writing, formatting, uploading. Then the work is done. The asset you created keeps selling long after you've moved on to the next project. And as your catalog grows, those individual royalties can start stacking into meaningful cash flow.

Better yet, you maintain control. You set the pricing. You decide whether to publish digitally, in print, or both. You can adjust based on performance, test different price points, or run promotions to spike visibility. And Amazon's reach, with its millions of active buyers, means you're not just selling to a local audience. You're tapping into global demand with zero extra infrastructure.

For investors, this isn't just convenient; it's strategic. Because once a book has traction, it becomes an asset that earns while you sleep, and scales without needing more of your time.

That's the kind of return that starts to feel a lot like owning equity in a business. One that just happens to be built on ideas instead of inventory.

Amazon Ads: Fuel for the Flywheel

One of the biggest advantages of publishing through Amazon KDP, and something many first-time authors overlook, is the access you get to Amazon's built-in marketing tools.

Unlike most platforms, where you're left to figure out traffic on your own, Amazon wants your book to sell. Why? Because when you earn, they earn. That alignment is powerful, and it's why the tools they offer can be such a valuable lever for authors and investors alike.

With Amazon Ads, you can run targeted campaigns that put your book directly in front of readers already browsing similar titles. You can also take advantage of free promotion days (if your book is enrolled in Kindle Unlimited) or offer limited-time discounts to boost visibility. These tools aren't just for driving sales; they're designed to help your book rank.

And ranking matters. A well-ranked book gets more organic visibility. More visibility means more clicks, which leads to more reviews, which feeds back into better rankings. This is what investors call a flywheel, a self-reinforcing loop that, once it's in motion, can keep spinning with little additional effort.

The beautiful part? Once the momentum is there, your role becomes more passive. You're no longer pushing the boulder uphill; the system is doing the work for you. New readers discover your book organically. Reviews trickle in. Sales continue, even if you're focused on your next project.

Of course, like any marketing, Amazon Ads come with a learning curve. It takes a few reps to figure out what's working and where the returns are. But once you dial in your strategy, and especially if you're managing a portfolio of books, the return on ad spend can be substantial.

For investors, that's the dream: a marketing engine that not only boosts revenue, but does it inside a platform that's already optimized for conversions. No need to build your own store, figure out traffic channels, or juggle five different dashboards.

Amazon brings the audience. You bring the content. Their ad tools help bridge the gap.

Done right, it's not just about advertising. It's about accelerating cash flow, building defensibility, and letting the machine work for you.

Where the Moats Show Up

Just like in the stock market, not all KDP businesses are created equal. Some are speculative, shiny new titles that haven't been tested by time. Others are built on real, durable advantages. The best KDP portfolios come with moats, structural features that protect revenue, reduce risk, and make the business harder to copy.

These moats matter. Because while almost anyone can upload a book, few can build a catalog that earns steadily for years. That consistency, that quiet compounding, is what separates a hobby from a real asset.

One of the clearest signs of a moat is a long sales history.

If a book or series has been generating consistent royalties for several months (and even years), you're not buying a bet; you're buying proof. That kind of track record shows the book has survived algorithm changes, seasonal shifts, and new competition. It tells you readers are still finding value, and that the content is still relevant. In an uncertain digital landscape, a long tail of sales is one of the most valuable signals you can find.

Another powerful moat? Reviews.

Thousands of high-quality, organic reviews, especially those averaging 4.5 stars or higher, are nearly impossible to replicate overnight. Social proof is a fortress. Anyone can copy your book's title, mimic your cover design, or even write similar content. But what they can't do is manufacture hundreds or thousands of verified readers, saying, "This book helped me," or "This series is worth every penny."

In the KDP ecosystem, reviews don't just boost conversion rates; they shape visibility. Strong reviews help books rank higher, show up more often in recommendation engines, and convert browsers into buyers. They're not just nice to have. They're a competitive advantage.

Niche domination is another form of defensibility.

Some authors carve out territory in specific genres: clean romance, personal finance for teens, Spanish-language workbooks for kids. If you own that niche, if readers associate your name or brand with what they're looking for, you've built a fanbase that keeps coming back. And in publishing, returning readers are gold. One good book becomes three. A three-book series becomes a full back catalog. And word of mouth starts doing the marketing for you.

Finally, keyword rankings are perhaps the most underestimated moat of all.

If your book ranks on the first page for a high-intent search like "budget planner for moms" or "beginner guitar chords," you've built digital real estate that can generate traffic passively. Those spots are earned through relevance, sales velocity, and click-through rates. And they're hard to take away. Just like a great location for a retail store, a top-ranking keyword gives you visibility that compounds over time.

Amazon has thousands of categories and thousands of bestsellers. But reaching the top of those lists, and staying there, takes real work. You can't fake momentum, and once you have it, it acts as a shield.

For investors, these moats are more than just nice features. They're what creates durability. They're what allows a KDP business to keep earning while you focus on growth, new acquisitions, or the next deal. Because in the end, the goal isn't just to buy a book. It's to own an asset, one with staying power, cash flow, and a competitive edge that lasts.

But There Are Real Risks

Now, for the part, Buffett would call the "what can go wrong" checklist.

First, the same low barrier to entry that makes KDP attractive also brings fierce competition. Anyone can publish a book. Some titles are created in a day, especially low-content books like journals or coloring books. That means even strong-performing books can face new threats at any time.

There's also ranking volatility. Your book might rank well today, but fall tomorrow due to algorithm shifts, review changes, or a competitor launching a better version. There's no "shelf space" guarantee like there is in physical bookstores.

Revenue concentration is another red flag. If 80% of the business income comes from one or two books, that's a fragile business. A drop in rankings or a policy issue with that book can have an outsized impact.

And then there's platform dependence. With KDP, Amazon is the gatekeeper. You don't own the customer. You don't control the algorithm. One policy change can shrink your margins or restrict your visibility overnight. You're playing on Amazon's turf, and they can change the rules anytime.

Finally, copyright issues can creep in, especially if you're managing a portfolio with multiple authors or ghostwriters. Keeping clean records and making sure everything is original is crucial to avoid takedowns or legal headaches.

Final Thoughts: Quiet Machines, Real Assets

KDP businesses are like little machines. Quiet, efficient, and often overlooked. When they're built right, with high-quality books, strong reviews, and rankings that hold, they can hum along in the background, producing steady cash flow month after month with very little ongoing effort.

They don't demand your full attention. They don't require a warehouse or a team. But they do reward thoughtfulness. And they do punish carelessness.

Like any machine, they need to be inspected before you turn the key. That means looking beyond surface-level numbers. Are the reviews authentic? Is the revenue spread across multiple books, or propped up by one lucky hit? Are the niches competitive or carved out? Is there a clear track record of performance or just a short-term spike?

Look for portfolios with history, depth, and diversification. Spread across categories, formats, or income streams. Those layers act as insulation when the algorithm shifts or trends cool off. Be especially mindful of concentration risk, where one title, one keyword, or one revenue stream carries most of the weight. Because in digital publishing, fragility often hides behind inflated numbers.

And don't forget: KDP has a low barrier to entry; anyone can publish. That means the real edge isn't access. It's execution. Trust, content quality, and reputation become the true moats. A book with a loyal following, strong reviews, and clear value isn't easily replaced, even in a crowded market.

That's what makes the best KDP businesses feel almost Buffett-like: they're simple, understandable, cash-flowing machines that reward patience and discipline.

So take your time. Think like an owner. And when you find the right one, don't just buy a book; buy the system behind it. The one built to last.

Intermediate Business Models

The Marketplace Business Model: Owning the Bridge, Not the Goods

When you invest in a marketplace business, you're not in the business of selling your own products. You're in the business of connection. You create a platform, a digital meeting ground, where buyers and sellers come together to do business. And every time they do, you take a small cut.

Think of Etsy for handmade crafts, Airbnb for vacation rentals, or niche B2B exchanges where manufacturers source specialized parts. You're not the seller. You're not the buyer. You're the one who owns the bridge, the critical piece of infrastructure that both sides need to cross in order to transact.

And that's the brilliance of the model. You're not tied up in inventory. You don't have to deal with warehouses, shipping logistics, or product returns. Your focus is on three high-leverage areas: trust, traffic, and transactions.

Build trust by creating a safe, reliable environment for both parties. Drive traffic, so there's always fresh demand. Facilitate smooth transactions so people come back again and again. If you do those three things well, the marketplace can scale with far less friction than a traditional retail or product-based business.

The real magic shows up in the flywheel.

As more sellers join your platform, it becomes more valuable to buyers. As more buyers arrive, more sellers want to be there. And so the cycle feeds itself. This network effect, where growth fuels more growth, is what makes marketplace businesses so powerful when they hit critical mass.

Best of all, the monetization model is flexible and layered. You can charge a transaction fee, offer paid listings, run ads, upsell premium services, or offer subscription plans for power users. None of those require holding product. None of them ties up your capital. But all of them can stack together to create a high-margin, recurring revenue business with surprisingly low overhead.

From an investor's point of view, this is a compelling setup. You're not betting on a single product or trend. You're betting on a system, one that, if well-designed, becomes more valuable the longer it runs.

You're not trying to invent the next big thing. You're buying the toll booth on a well-traveled road. And once that bridge is built and trusted, people will keep crossing it. Every day. Every transaction. Without you having to carry the goods yourself.

Where Things Get Tricky

As attractive as the marketplace model is, it's not without its challenges. There's no such thing as a free lunch, and building or buying a marketplace that actually works takes more than just plugging in the tech.

The biggest hurdle? Traction.

If you're buying a marketplace that hasn't yet reached critical mass, be prepared for a grind. Marketplaces suffer from what's often called the chicken-and-egg problem: buyers won't show up unless there are sellers, and sellers won't list unless there are buyers. Until that loop gets going, it's a slow, often frustrating uphill battle.

Even once you're off the ground, the real work is in keeping the ecosystem balanced.

Too many sellers and not enough buyers? You'll end up with stale inventory, angry vendors, and low conversion rates. Too many buyers but not enough product or service providers? People bounce. Marketplaces don't scale in a straight line. They scale in cycles, and maintaining that two-sided equilibrium is one of the most operationally challenging parts of the whole model.

Then there's trust, the lifeblood of any marketplace.

Unlike a traditional product business where you control the inventory, marketplaces rely on third parties to deliver the goods or services. That means your brand is on the line for someone else's behavior. One unpleasant experience, such as a late shipment, a scam listing, or a fake profile, and your reputation takes a hit. Worse, that hit can go viral in hours. Rebuilding trust takes far longer and often costs real money.

You also have to watch for something called disintermediation, a fancy term for when buyers and sellers decide to cut you out of the deal. If your platform becomes nothing more than a matchmaking service with a fee, people will eventually ask themselves, "Why not just deal directly?"

It's a real problem, especially if the value you provide ends after the first transaction.

Take Upwork, for example. It connects freelancers and clients, but once that relationship is established, there's a real temptation to move off-platform and avoid the fees. Upwork knows this, which is why they've built features that go beyond just matchmaking. Things like payment protection, time tracking, easy dispute resolution, and, most importantly, access to more work. That ongoing value is what keeps users on the platform.

Or look at Zocdoc, which helps patients find and book doctors. You might think it's a one-and-done experience. But Zocdoc adds value well beyond the first appointment: real-time availability, verified reviews, insurance filtering, and appointment reminders all make the platform sticky. The more convenience and confidence they deliver, the harder it becomes to justify leaving.

The lesson? If you're going to own the bridge, you'd better make it worth crossing.

Great marketplaces succeed not just by connecting supply and demand, but by adding so much value on top of the connection that people don't want to, or can't afford to, go around it. That's your real moat. If you can build or buy a platform that nails that balance, you're no longer just a middleman. You're infrastructure.

But it's not easy. And it's definitely not passive. You'll need systems, support, and smart oversight. Because when a marketplace works, it really works. But getting there and staying there takes discipline, not just vision.

What Makes a Marketplace Defensible

When a marketplace business starts to click, when supply and demand find rhythm and transactions flow consistently, something important begins to happen beneath the surface: moats start to form.

And moats, as Buffett would say, are what protect a business from competition and help it keep earning year after year.

The biggest moat in a successful marketplace? Network effects.

This is when the value of the platform grows with every new user. More sellers attract more buyers. More buyers bring in more sellers. The whole thing starts compounding. And once your platform becomes the place where your niche audience gathers, whether it's for hiring freelancers, booking services, or sourcing hard-to-find parts, it becomes incredibly hard for a newcomer to replicate that momentum from scratch.

Competitors may copy your interface or pricing, but they can't manufacture a thriving ecosystem overnight. That community, that liquidity of supply and demand, becomes your defensive wall.

Then there's stickiness, especially on the seller side.

Sellers invest in your platform. They build out profiles, collect reviews, and work their way into the algorithm. They start getting regular traffic, sales, and repeat customers. That takes time, and they're not eager to start over on a brand-new site unless the upside is massive and immediate.

This creates switching costs, not the kind you see on a balance sheet, but the kind that matter deeply in digital businesses. Sellers don't just want to leave. They don't need to. And that inertia works in your favor.

Another powerful edge? Data.

As the marketplace operator, you see everything. What's selling, when it's selling, how much people are willing to pay, and where the gaps are. That visibility lets you make informed, strategic moves that outsiders can't.

Maybe you spot a fast-growing category and launch your own white-label product. Maybe you see pricing inefficiencies and adjust commission structures to increase volume. Or maybe you use that data to feed smarter ad targeting, cross-promotions, or premium features.

The point is: data compounds. And once you have enough of it, you start seeing opportunities others can't even spot, let alone act on.

And finally, there's brand trust. The softest, but maybe most important moat of all.

If buyers associate your name with selection, safety, and quality, they'll keep coming back. If sellers trust that your platform delivers traffic, protects payments, and resolves issues fairly, they'll stay loyal. That kind of trust can't be bought. It has to be earned through consistency, fairness, and time.

And once you've earned it, it becomes the hardest thing for competitors to steal.

So while marketplaces may start as simple tech platforms, the great ones evolve into something far more powerful: ecosystems with built-in defensibility. A strong brand. A deep pool of users. Data advantages. And switching costs that make it easier to stay than to leave.

That's when you stop being just a connector and start becoming infrastructure.

And that, from an investor's perspective, is where the real value lives.

Final Word

Marketplace businesses can be great, especially when they're firing on all cylinders. No inventory, strong margins, and built-in scalability make them appealing on paper. And if you've got real network effects and brand trust, you can build something defensible over time.

But here's the reality: they're not passive. You're stepping into a business where you have to keep both buyers and sellers happy, deal with disputes, manage customer service, and constantly watch for things like fraud or platform abuse. It's not just owning a website; it's running an ecosystem.

That's the reason I don't invest in this space. I prefer models that are more hands-off once they're up and running. With marketplaces, the operational load tends to stick around. And truthfully, it's hard to find smaller online marketplaces that truly have a strong network effect or durable moat. Most never get to critical mass; they're stuck in the middle, with just enough activity to be frustrating but not enough to fly.

The best ones build momentum. The rest end up spinning their wheels.

If you're looking at a deal in this space, make sure you see signs of a real flywheel, a diverse revenue base, and high user trust. If those aren't obvious, you might not be buying a bridge. You might just be standing in traffic.

What's Outside My Circle (And Maybe Yours Too)

I personally focus mainly on content businesses and Amazon KDP. Why? Because, compared to other models, they're relatively passive and easier to manage. Once they're up and running, they don't demand daily firefighting. That gives me more time to think and less time stuck in the weeds.

That said, I always keep an eye out for the right kind of marketplace business. The kind with a moat and within my budget. I haven't pulled the trigger on one yet, but when the right opportunity comes along, I will and want to learn and expand my circle of confidence.

However, not every business model is a fit, and that's okay. One of the most valuable lessons I've learned as an investor is knowing what not to chase, even if it looks shiny from the outside.

There are a few types of businesses I steer clear of. Not because they're bad; in fact, some of them can be incredibly lucrative. But because they don't align with the kind of work I enjoy, the lifestyle I want, or the skill set I'm building over the long haul.

In other words, they fall outside my circle of competence.

Social Media Brands

Buying a popular YouTube channel or an influencer's Instagram account might seem like a shortcut to passive income. But the truth is, most of the time, the brand is the person. The audience is loyal not to the content alone, but also to the personality behind it: their voice, their face, their story.

And unless you're that person, or can convincingly replace them, the trust doesn't transfer. Engagement drops, views fade, and what looked like a thriving channel can slowly lose its magic. I'd rather own something where the asset carries the value, not the personality attached to it.

Ecommerce

Selling physical products sounds simple. Buy low, sell high. What could go wrong?

Plenty.

Inventory headaches, returns, damaged shipments, customer service nightmares, platform policy changes... the list is long. Margins are often thinner than they look, and cash flow can get tight if you're constantly reinvesting in stock. Add in logistics, supply chain delays, and the operational complexity of fulfilling orders at scale, and suddenly your "passive" side hustle feels more like a full-time job.

Unless you're already deep in the trenches of physical product ops, or you love managing details, this model can be a grind.

SaaS (Software as a Service)

On paper, SaaS is the holy grail: recurring revenue, high margins, global scalability. What's not to like?

But here's the catch: Software breaks. Bugs pop up. APIs change. Servers crash. And when something goes wrong (and it will), you can't just Google your way out of it. You need technical chops. Either you write code yourself, or you've got a developer you trust on speed dial.

If you're non-technical like me, that creates real exposure. You're depending on someone else to keep the wheels turning. And that's fine if you've built those relationships and systems. But if not, you're flying blind in a space where response time matters.

Could someone else succeed wildly with these models? Absolutely. I've seen it happen.

But for me, the goal isn't to chase every opportunity. It's to focus on the ones where I can bring judgment, experience, and a calm hand. The kind of edge that compounds.

So take this not as a warning, but as a reminder: the best investments aren't always the flashiest. They're the ones that fit. And knowing what to walk away from is just as important as knowing what to pursue.

Chapter Four

Where the Deals Are: Hunting Grounds for Online Business Buyers

Marketplace Overview

L ET'S START WITH THE lay of the land: the main platforms where online businesses are bought and sold and what each one is best suited for. I regularly check three marketplaces. You don't have to pick just one. It's like browsing different shelves at the same store. Each has its own flavor.

Empire Flippers

Empire Flippers is like walking into a well-run dealership instead of browsing Craigslist. You're still buying a used car, but it's been cleaned up, inspected, and the guy handing you the keys probably has a name badge and a business card.

Most of the listings you'll find on Empire Flippers sit in that sweet spot, not tiny side projects, but not billion-dollar unicorns either. Think $50K to a few million. That's where the action is for serious individual investors or small funds. And because they vet both the sellers and the businesses, you're less likely to stumble into a digital lemon.

I've personally looked through hundreds of listings across different platforms, and Empire Flippers always felt more trustworthy. The numbers are organized. The seller interviews are clear. If you ask a question, someone actually answers. That kind of support makes a difference, especially when you're wiring six figures for a business you've never physically touched.

Charlie Munger once said, "Show me the incentive and I'll show you the outcome." Empire Flippers gets paid only when a deal closes, and that incentive aligns them with both sides. They want clean deals that go through, not endless tire-kicking. That pushes them to filter out the junk early.

Of course, you still need to do your homework. But starting with a tighter pool of quality businesses? That's half the battle won already.

Flippa

Now, Flippa is more of a Wild West and is like a flea market for online businesses. You might find a hidden gem, but you'll step over a dozen broken toasters and fake Rolexes to get there.

You've got everything under one roof: $500 content sites that haven't made a dollar, sitting right next to $2 million SaaS businesses with teams and traction. That variety can be exciting, especially if you're early in your journey and just want to poke around. But it also means you've got to be sharp. The platform doesn't vet listings like Empire Flippers does. Some sellers are honest. Others are creative with their accounting.

I've seen listings claiming "passive income" that turned out to be anything but. One guy listed a content site making $2K a month. It looked good on paper. But after a little digging, I realized most of the traffic was from one Reddit post that went viral six months ago. That's not a business; that's lightning in a bottle.

Flippa's strength is its speed and openness. Deals move quickly. You can message sellers directly. You can make offers below asking. It's less polished, but if you know what to look for, and you're okay with sifting through the noise, there's value to be had. It's where you go hunting with a flashlight, not where you expect a guided tour.

If you understand how websites make money, how to verify traffic and revenue, and you're comfortable saying no a lot, Flippa can work for you. But if you're just starting out and want something safe and tidy, you might want to look elsewhere first.

Motion Invest

Motion Invest is probably the easiest place to start if you're new to buying online businesses. It's beginner-friendly by design; everything from the types of sites listed to the way the deals are structured is made to keep things simple.

They focus only on content sites, usually in the $5K to $100K range. These are mostly blogs or niche sites that earn through display ads, Amazon affiliate links, or other passive-ish income streams. No complicated tech, no customer support headaches, no inventory. Just traffic and content, which makes them easier to understand and manage, especially if you're not coming from a technical background.

The listings are fewer, but the big advantage is that they're all vetted in-house. Motion Invest does their own due diligence before a site even hits the marketplace. That means fewer junk listings, less time wasted chasing down fake numbers, and a smoother experience overall. You still need to do your homework, but it's more like reviewing a used car with a Carfax report already printed out for you.

I've gone to Motion Invest when I wanted to scoop up a small site quickly. Maybe I had some extra cash sitting around. Maybe I wanted to test a niche or try a new monetization strategy. These sites won't change your life overnight, but they can bring in a few hundred or a few thousand dollars a month if you pick wisely and put in a bit of work.

It's a great starting point for folks who want to learn by doing. Buy a smaller site, run it, grow it a little, and get familiar with how content sites actually make money. You don't need to be an expert. You just need to be willing to learn.

So here's the takeaway: Empire Flippers is where I go for scale and clean, high-quality deals. Flippa is the wild west — high risk, high reward, if you know what you're doing. And Motion Invest? That's where you start small, stay safe, and get some experience under your belt. I keep an eye on all three, because you never know where the next great deal will show up.

Deal Flow & Quality

Empire Flippers is all about quality over quantity. You won't see dozens of new deals every day, but the ones that do make it through have already been vetted: traffic, earnings, operations, the whole nine yards. If it's listed, it's passed a pretty high bar.

Flippa is the opposite. Tons of listings, all the time. New sites pop up daily. Blogs, apps, SaaS, you name it. Some are great, and some are, let's just say, "optimistically presented." You've got to do your own homework and double-check everything.

Motion Invest sits somewhere in the middle. The volume is lower than Flippa, but every site gets reviewed by their team before it goes live. So while you won't find a flood of deals, you're not wasting time sorting through junk, either.

Bottom line? Empire Flippers = fewer, higher-quality listing s. Flippa = more deals, but more digging. Motion Invest = a nice balance. Fewer listings, but cleaner and verified.

Due Diligence Support

This is where the differences between platforms really show up.

Empire Flippers gives you the most support. Before you even talk to a seller, they've already verified the traffic, the revenue, and pulled together a full profit-and-loss statement. Once you're in the buying process, their team stays with you all the way through. It's about as close to white-glove service as you'll find in this space.

Flippa is more of a DIY setup. Sellers upload their own numbers, and while some listings get vetted, many don't. They do offer tools to help, and they've added a buyer protection option, kind of like insurance, in case you get misled in a material way. But still, the burden of proof is on you. If you're confident in your own due diligence, it can work well. If not, you could miss something important.

Motion Invest lands somewhere in the middle. They verify traffic and earnings before listing a site, but the process is light-touch. No detailed walkthroughs, but no major red flags either. You get a cleaner experience than Flippa, but you won't get the hand-holding Empire Flippers offers.

So here's the rule of thumb:If you want full support, go with Empire Flippers.If you're comfortable doing the digging yourself, Flippa and Motion Invest are solid. Just make sure you understand what you are walking into.

Pricing & Fees

Let's talk about how each platform handles money: what it costs to buy and how the fees are structured.

Empire Flippers doesn't charge buyers a fee, but you'll need to put down a refundable deposit if you want to unlock full listing details. That's their way of filtering for serious buyers. Sellers pay a commission, usually between 10% and 15%, which is built into the final deal price.

Flippa is a little more open. No buyer fees [or monthly fees to get early listing access]. No deposit required. Sellers pay a listing fee upfront and a success fee when their business sells. It's easy to browse and jump into deals, but you're also on your own more.

Motion Invest is the most beginner-friendly when it comes to cost. No fees, no deposits, and most listings fall under $100K. It's a great entry point if you're working with a smaller budget and want something simple and low-pressure.

There are definitely other marketplaces out there: Investors Club, BizBuySell, Acquire.com, SideProjectors, and a handful more that pop up now and then. Each has its niche. Some are better for SaaS. Some focus on e-commerce. Others are more like classified ads where anything goes.

But when it comes to content sites and Amazon KDP businesses, the kinds of digital assets that are relatively low-maintenance and cash flow-friendly, I keep circling back to just three: Empire Flippers, Flippa, and Motion Invest.

They each have their own flavor. Empire Flippers gives you polished, vetted listings with solid financials. Flippa's the hustle-heavy marketplace where you need to dig, but the range is unbeatable. Motion Invest is streamlined, simple, and built for smaller content sites that are easy to understand and operate.

What I like is that, together, they hit the right mix of quality, transparency, and ease of use. No marketplace is perfect. There are always risks. Sellers stretch the truth. Numbers don't always tell the full story. But between these three, you've got enough tools, enough variety, and enough built-in filtering to find good opportunities, if you're patient and know what to look for.

Personally, I check all three pretty regularly. I'm not looking for perfection. I'm looking for value, something underpriced, overlooked, or just well-positioned for growth. And every now and then, one of these platforms serves it up. You just have to be ready when it does.

Chapter Five

Stay in Your Lane. Your Circle of Competence in the Digital Age

C HARLIE MUNGER ONCE SAID, "I look for a place where I'm wise and they're stupid." It sounds a little blunt, but he's right. The best investors don't try to outplay everyone at everything. They focus on where they've got the edge. Where they understand the rules of the game, and others don't.

That's what your circle of competence is all about. It's not about knowing everything; it's about knowing what you know and staying close to that. This is especially true when investing in online businesses.

Think of it this way. The internet is full of shiny objects: dropshipping, SaaS, YouTube automation, KDP, niche content sites. Every now and then, there's a new "hot model." But chasing everything is a great way to master nothing. And when you're buying or running a business, that's dangerous.

You don't need to be an expert in every business model. You just need to be honest about which ones you truly understand and which ones you don't. For me, content businesses and Amazon KDP fall squarely in my circle. I've spent time in the trenches with them. I know how they work, where they break, and how to fix them. Other models? Not so much. I stay away.

You'll need to do the same kind of gut check. Not everything will click with you, and that's okay. The key is to figure out which types of businesses actually make sense to you. The kind you can look at and say, "Yeah, I get how this works." Then ask yourself, "Am I willing to put in the time to get better at this? Can I see myself learning the ropes, solving problems, and sticking with it when it gets tough?"

It's also worth thinking about whether you've got, or can realistically build, the skills needed to run that type of business well. And don't ignore the practical stuff: how much time do you really have? What kind of budget are you working with? A business might look great on paper, but if it doesn't fit your life, it's not in your circle.

This isn't about putting limits on yourself. It's about putting yourself in a position to win. Buffett puts it well: "The size of your circle of competence isn't very important. Knowing its boundaries, however, is vital."

The best opportunities aren't always the flashiest ones. They're the ones where you know the terrain better than most and can make good decisions because of it.

Matching Your Goals with Your Circle of Competence

Before you go shopping for an online business, it's worth taking a hard look in the mirror. Not just at what you want, but at what you can realistically manage, based on your life, your goals, and your circle of competence.

Buying even a small business is a real commitment. It's not like buying a stock where you click a button and forget about it. It takes attention. Time. Sometimes frustration. So before jumping into listings, ask yourself: are you trying to replace a full-time income, or just build a side hustle?

If your goal is full-time income, you'll need to be in the weeds early on. You've got to understand the engine before you can let someone else drive. That means picking a business you're comfortable running day to day, not just something that looks good on a spreadsheet. It has to fall within your circle. Otherwise, you'll either get overwhelmed or bored, and neither leads to good outcomes.

But if you're like me, working a 9-to-5 with a family and a packed calendar, then you're probably leaning toward side income. In that case, your circle of competence should include not just the business model, but your ability to manage it without becoming a bottleneck. I look for businesses that run on 5 hours a week or less. I've built systems. I've learned what to automate, what to outsource, and what to simply not do. It's worked well so far. I've got a young son, a full-time job, and a portfolio of stocks and online businesses that don't need me babysitting them.

The bottom line is this: your goals shape what "competence" looks like. A great business for one person might be a terrible fit for another. It's not just about what the business earns. It's about whether you can run it well without it running you into the ground.

Know Your Budget, and Stay Within It

Let's talk about money for a minute. Not just how much you want to spend, but what you can actually afford comfortably. One of the fastest ways to get in trouble with an online business is to stretch your budget so far that you leave yourself no margin for error.

So before making any offers, get clear on two numbers: your top-end acquisition price and how much extra you can set aside for growth. Buying the business is just step one. After that, there's almost always some kind of investment needed, whether it's SEO help, fresh content, a website redesign, or paid ads to jumpstart traffic. If you blow your entire budget on the purchase, you'll be running on fumes the second something unexpected pops up. And it will pop up.

This is where your financial circle of competence comes in. You need to stay within it. It's not just about understanding businesses; it's about knowing your own risk tolerance. If you're nervous about spending $30K on a business, don't kid yourself into thinking you'll feel fine spending another $10K a few weeks later. Keep dry powder. Give yourself room to breathe.

A solid business bought at a price you can't afford is no longer a solid business. It's a ticking time bomb. Stay within your circle, financially and operationally, and you'll sleep a lot better at night.

Know Your Skills and What You're Willing to Learn

Warren Buffett once said, "Investing in yourself is the best thing you can do. Anything that improves your own talents; nobody can tax it or take it away from you." That advice matters just as much in online business as it does in investing.

You don't need to show up knowing everything. I sure didn't. But you do need to be clear on where you're starting from and what you're actually willing to learn. Some folks get excited about the idea of owning an online business, right up until they realize it involves figuring out SEO or hiring freelancers. That's when reality shows up and says, "Hey, this might not be my game."

Your circle of competence includes your current skills, but also the skills you're open to developing. For me, keyword research has been the single most important skill in my playbook, both for content sites and for Amazon KDP. It's not rocket science, but it does take some practice. Understanding what people are searching for, and how to position content to match that intent, is the foundation for everything else.

Once you've got a feel for that, SEO comes next. Whether you're optimizing blog posts for Google or fine-tuning a book listing on Amazon, knowing how to structure titles, tweak descriptions, and build authority can make a massive difference. Again, learnable, but only if you're willing to roll up your sleeves.

Same goes for digital marketing. You don't have to become an ad wizard overnight, but getting a working knowledge of how to attract attention, through Google ads, social media, or Amazon's ad platform, will give you leverage.

And finally, don't underestimate the power of delegation. Learning how to use platforms like Upwork or Fiverr to outsource tasks without losing control? That's a skill too. And one that can buy back your time fast.

We'll dig deeper into all of this later in the due diligence chapters. For now, just ask yourself: "Which of these skills am I already comfortable with? Which ones feel within reach? And which ones make me want to run for the hills?"

That's how you draw the edge of your operating circle. The sharper that line, the fewer surprises you'll have when it's time to actually run the business.

Chapter Six

Kicking the Tires: Content Site Due Diligence

"R ISK COMES FROM NOT knowing what you're doing."
—Warren Buffett

Buying a content site can be one of the smartest ways to build real, semi-passive income, the kind that keeps working while you sleep. But only if you know how to tell a good deal from a bad one. The internet's full of pretty-looking websites that fall apart the second you peek under the hood.

This chapter is all about helping you avoid those traps. I'll walk you through how to vet a deal before you even talk to a seller, and what to ask once you're in the conversation. That way, you won't waste weeks chasing a site that was never going to work in the first place.

You might be thinking a content site isn't quite what you're looking for. But here's the thing: whether or not you plan to own one, the skills you learn from running a content site are foundational. They belong in your toolkit no matter what kind of online business you choose.

Whether it's KDP, SaaS, a marketplace, or something else entirely, if you don't know how to drive traffic, you're flying blind. Understanding how content attracts, converts, and compounds over time is a core skill for any digital operator. So don't skip over the Content Site 101. Treat it as the groundwork. Because once you've got traffic figured out, everything else gets easier.

What to Do *Before* You Ever Meet the Seller

Before you hop on a call or send a message to a seller, there's a lot you can and should figure out on your own. In fact, you should be able to screen out 90% of bad deals without ever talking to anyone. That alone will save you hours of wasted conversations.

When I first started, this pre-screening process felt like climbing a mountain. I'd spend three, sometimes four, hours digging into a listing. But like anything else, it gets easier. These days, I can rule out the duds in a couple of minutes, and for the ones that pass the sniff test, a deeper initial review takes maybe 20 to 30 minutes. That speed becomes a huge advantage over time. The more deals you screen, the faster your pattern recognition builds. What used to feel like detective work starts to feel like instinct.

Buffett put it perfectly: "I have some filters in my mind, so if somebody calls me about an investment, I usually know in two or three minutes whether I have an interest." That's the mindset you want to develop: quick filters, clear red flags, no guilt about moving on fast. The goal is to protect your time and focus on the deals that actually have potential.

As you go through your initial due diligence, make notes. Write down every question that pops up, whether it's about traffic, monetization, backlinks, or how the seller runs the site day to day. If the site passes your pre-check, you'll use that list when you talk to the seller. And because you've done your homework, that conversation will be sharper, more focused, and way more valuable.

Think of this early work as sharpening your axe before chopping wood. The better your process, the fewer bad trees you'll waste time swinging at.

Use Marketplace Filters and Read Listings Like a Detective

When you're browsing deals on platforms like Flippa, Empire Flippers, or Motion Invest, the first step is to let the filters do some heavy lifting for you. These marketplaces give you tools to sort through the noise. Use them.

I always filter by asking price to stay within my budget. Then I zero in on listings with positive monthly cash flow. If a site isn't making money now, I don't assume I'll magically turn it around later. That's not investing. That's wishful thinking.

Site age is another big one for me. I usually set the minimum at one year. Why? Because I want to see at least 12 months of traffic and financial history. A site that's only been live for three months might be a flash in the pan. A year gives me a clearer picture of whether it's stable or just got lucky once.

Once I've narrowed things down, I read the listing like a detective. I don't just skim; I ask myself: "If I were a visitor to this site, what value would I actually get from it? Is it solving a real problem? Is the content any good?"

Then I look at how the site makes money. Is it through display ads, affiliate links, or digital products? Does that revenue model make sense given the niche?

And finally, I keep my radar up for anything that feels vague or off. Big claims about traffic or earnings without clear proof? Vague language about how the site's been "passively managed" but somehow growing fast? Those are yellow flags. Sometimes red.

You're not trying to find the perfect deal here. You're trying to avoid wasting time on ones that don't pass the smell test. The goal is to get sharper with every listing you read. Over time, you'll start spotting patterns: the good, the bad, and the too-good-to-be-true.

Ask for Read-Only Access to Google Analytics

This one's not optional. If a seller won't give you read-only access to their Google Analytics, that's a deal breaker. Plain and simple. You want real data, not a screenshot dressed up to look good.

Here's how I usually approach it. I start by checking traffic using SEO tools like Semrush or Ahrefs. Those are great for getting a rough idea of trends, whether traffic is growing, flat, or tanking. But they're still just estimates. They can miss things. So if a site looks promising, the next step is always to ask for read-only access to Google Analytics. How? You can send one message to the seller for this with your email address on whichever marketplace you are in.

That's where you get the truth. Actual visitor numbers. Real traffic sources. Country breakdowns. Device types. Bounce rate. All the stuff that tells you whether this site has a real audience or just a few random clicks.

It also shows you whether the traffic is consistent or spiky. A traffic spike from a Reddit post six months ago might make the numbers look good, but it doesn't mean the site is healthy.

Once I've done my initial check and the site still looks interesting, I don't hesitate. I message the seller and ask for GA access. Sellers usually expect this, and some sites, like Motion Invest, provide it with a click of a mouse, even without the need to contact the seller.

Dig into the Site with Google Analytics, Ahrefs, or Semrush

Once a listing catches your eye, that's not the finish line; that's the starting gate. The photos might look good, the numbers might sparkle, but until you peek behind the curtain, you're really just guessing.

This is where tools like Google Analytics, Ahrefs, or Semrush come in. Think of them as your due diligence toolkit, like getting a home inspection before you buy the house. They give you X-ray vision. You're not just trusting the seller's story anymore. You're checking the actual data to see if it holds up.

Google Analytics tells you who's visiting the site, where they're coming from, and what they're doing once they get there. Is the traffic steady or spiky? Is it mostly organic, or is the seller buying traffic and calling it growth? You can spot red flags fast if you know where to look.

Website Traffic

When I'm evaluating a potential deal, I always start with traffic. It's the lifeblood of any content site. Without it, the business is dead on arrival. I want to understand not just how much traffic a site is getting, but also how that traffic has been trending over time. Is it growing? Flat? Or on a slow, steady decline?

I tend to gravitate toward sites with flat or growing traffic. Sure, they're usually more expensive, but there's a reason for that. A consistent or rising audience is one of the clearest signals that the site is still relevant, useful, and ranking well. And in this game, consistency is underrated. It gives you a steady foundation to build on, rather than starting in a hole and trying to dig your way out.

Now, if traffic is declining, I don't immediately walk away, but it does raise my eyebrows. I make a mental note to ask the seller about it. Sometimes there's a good reason. Maybe they stopped posting content a year ago, or maybe Google rolled out an algorithm update that clipped their wings. That's the kind of thing I want to understand before moving forward. Can it be fixed? If so, how much time and money will it take? Because declining traffic often means declining revenue, and you need to know what you're walking into.

A good example: I once came across a site in the travel niche that was earning decent money but had lost half its traffic over the past six months. The seller blamed seasonality, claiming traffic always dipped after summer. But when I looked at historical data, that didn't hold up. What really happened was a Google update hit their top-ranking posts. Their backlinks were weak, and the content hadn't been updated in years. If I hadn't dug in, I might've bought a sinking ship.

Speaking of seasonality, that's another thing I always look for. Some niches are tied closely to the calendar. Think gardening in the spring, fitness in January, or Halloween costumes in October. A traffic spike might look like growth, but if it's tied to a one-time seasonal surge, that changes the story. It's not a deal-breaker, but you want to understand the rhythm. I've seen listings that looked like they were on fire, massive jumps in traffic, only to realize it was from one good month tied to Black Friday. You buy that site in February and wonder where all the visitors went.

Next, I dig into where the traffic is coming from. The source matters. A lot. If a big chunk of visitors are typing in the site's URL directly, what we call *direct traffic*, that's a great sign. It means the site has a real following. People remember it, trust it, and come back without needing to be reminded. That kind of loyalty is hard to fake.

Organic traffic from search engines is another strong pillar, especially if it comes from a broad base of keywords. But you want to make sure it's not overly reliant on just one or two blog posts. I've seen sites making five figures a month from a single ranking. Great while it lasts, until Google sneezes and you're wiped off the map.

Then there's *paid traffic*. This is where I get cautious. If the seller is buying traffic through Facebook ads, Google Ads, or native ad networks, you have to understand the economics inside and out. How much are they spending? What's the return? How sustainable is it? Because the second you stop feeding that ad machine, the traffic and the business can dry up overnight.

Geography is another piece that often gets overlooked. Not all traffic is created equal. Early on in my investing journey, I found a content site pulling in over two million visits a month. It was monetized through display ads and listed for under $40,000. I thought I'd struck gold. But when I opened up the analytics, I realized the bulk of the traffic came from India and Southeast Asia. Nothing wrong with that, but for display ads, especially with networks like Mediavine or AdThrive, U.S. traffic earns significantly more. Sometimes 5–10x more per visitor. Once I adjusted for revenue per thousand impressions (RPM), the deal didn't pencil out. The surface-level numbers looked great, but the value wasn't there.

So yeah, traffic isn't just a number. It's a story. Where it's coming from, how it's trending, and what it's made of, all shape the quality of the business underneath. You don't need to be an SEO expert to figure this stuff out. But you do need to be curious. Ask questions. Look under the hood. And don't be afraid to walk away if the story doesn't make sense.

Website Visitor Engagement

Once I've got a handle on traffic trends, I shift gears and dig into engagement, because traffic alone doesn't pay the bills. It's what visitors do once they land on the site that really tells you what kind of business you're dealing with.

I start with the basics: How long are people staying? Are they reading one page and bouncing, or are they clicking around and exploring? How many pages per visit? What's the bounce rate? These numbers might sound a bit dry, but they tell a powerful story about user experience. Imagine you're running a bookstore. People walk in, glance at the shelves, and walk right back out. That's high bounce rate, low engagement. But if they wander in, grab a coffee, sit down with a book, and stick around for a while? That's engagement. And in the world of online business, it usually means your content is doing its job.

I once looked at a health blog that had steady traffic, but the average session duration was under 30 seconds. Most visitors read a single post and left. No email opt-ins. No clicks to other pages. No affiliate conversions. The site looked healthy at first glance, but it wasn't holding attention. And if you're not keeping eyeballs on the page, it's hard to monetize, especially with ads or affiliate links, which rely on clicks and time spent.

On the flip side, I reviewed a parenting site where people were spending over four minutes per session and visiting three or more pages. That's excellent. The content was practical, well-written, and deeply targeted to a specific audience: new moms looking for real advice. That kind of engagement not only boosts your SEO rankings (Google notices when users stick around), but it also sets the stage for stronger monetization. Display ads perform better.

Affiliate links get clicked. Email lists grow faster. Everything gets easier when the site is sticky.

Engagement also hints at trust. If someone reads multiple articles, chances are they view the site as credible. That opens the door for things like digital products, sponsorships, or community building down the road. But if the site is just a revolving door of quick visits, it's probably missing that trust factor, and that limits your upside.

One metric I love is "average time on page." If it's high, that means people are actually reading, not just skimming and leaving. I don't need viral numbers here. Even a modest niche site with strong engagement can be a goldmine. You don't need millions of visits a month if the ones you do get are loyal, engaged, and converting.

Bottom line: engagement metrics tell you if people care. And when people care, the business has a pulse. I'd take a smaller site with deep engagement over a high-traffic site with shallow behavior any day. Because depth creates value, and value is what you're really buying.

Keyword rankings

Keyword rankings are one of the most telling signs of a site's health and potential. After all, keywords are how people find a site in the first place. If traffic is the engine, keywords are the fuel.

When I'm evaluating a site, I always pull up its keyword profile using tools like Semrush or Ahrefs. I want to see what the site ranks for, where it ranks, and how stable those rankings are over time. This gives me a sense of whether the site is just lucky, ranking for one or two breakout posts, or if it has a deep bench of content pulling in traffic consistently.

The type of keywords a site ranks for also matters a ton. A site ranking for things like "best hiking backpacks for beginners" or "how to brew coffee at home" is playing in high-value territory. Those keywords have intent. People searching for them are often just one or two clicks away from pulling out their wallets. Whether it's through affiliate links, display ads, or digital products, that kind of traffic can translate directly into revenue.

Now compare that to a site ranking for trivia-style searches like "what year was coffee invented?" or "fun facts about hiking." That might drive traffic, but it's mostly curiosity clicks, which are harder to monetize and less predictable.

One site I looked at recently had thousands of ranking keywords, but most were low-intent terms. Tons of impressions, but almost no affiliate revenue. It was like owning a store with plenty of foot traffic. People would walk in, look around, and leave without buying anything. Flashy on the surface, but not great for the bottom line.

Another thing I watch closely is the trend. Are the keyword rankings going up, flat, or slipping? A site that's climbing in the rankings has tailwinds, especially if the niche still has room to grow. On the other hand, if a site is losing positions across the board, I want to know why. Maybe a Google update hit them. Maybe their content is outdated. Or maybe a stronger competitor entered the scene. Whatever it is, I need to understand the cause and whether it's fixable.

I also look at how many keywords the site ranks for in total. A site that ranks for a wide spread of keywords, even if most are in positions #11–30 (page 2 or 3 of Google), tells me there's potential. With a bit of optimization, those could easily move up to page 1, and the traffic could grow without creating much new content.

At the end of the day, keyword rankings are more than just numbers; they're the story of how a site is discovered. If that story is strong and built on valuable, relevant, intent-driven keywords, the site has a solid foundation. And if rankings are climbing? Even better. That's a sign the site hasn't peaked yet.

In short: I don't just want traffic. I want the right kind of traffic. And keyword rankings are where that story begins.

Domain Authority

After traffic, engagement, and keyword ranking, the next thing I look at is domain authority and how long the site has been around. These two go hand in hand, and together, they give you a sense of how much trust the site has built up in Google's eyes.

Domain Authority, or DA, is a score typically measured on a scale from 1 to 100 that estimates how likely a website is to rank in search results. It's not something Google publishes, but it's a widely used metric developed by tools like Semrush and Ahrefs. The score reflects things like backlinks, referring domains, and the overall strength of the site's SEO footprint.

A high DA means the site has earned trust. Other websites are linking to it. Google sees it as legit. And in the world of search rankings, that trust goes a long way. It's like walking into a party and already knowing the host. You get in quicker and people take you more seriously.

I learned this the hard way. Early in my investing journey, I decided to build a site from scratch. I was excited. I put together strong content, designed a clean layout, even created digital products to sell. I did everything by the book. But the site didn't take off. Not even close. It sat in the SEO basement, getting barely a trickle of traffic. Why? Because the domain was brand new. My DA score was basically zero, and Google didn't trust me yet. It was like shouting into the void.

That experience taught me a simple lesson: momentum matters. A site with even a few years under its belt and some decent backlinks has a much easier time ranking, even if the content isn't amazing. Google tends to reward age and authority. It doesn't like newcomers until they've proven themselves. So rather than pushing a boulder uphill and hoping for traction, I'd rather buy a site that already has some wind at its back.

One deal I looked at recently had a DA in the mid-40s and had been around for seven years. The content was outdated, and the monetization was sloppy; the owner hadn't touched it in months. But that didn't scare me off. In fact, that's what made it interesting. Because under the hood, the site had built up trust. With a little cleanup (fresh articles, a better theme, some affiliate tweaks), it could easily bounce back. That's the kind of upside you're looking for.

So while DA isn't the only metric that matters, it's a solid proxy for how much effort has already gone into earning Google's trust. Combine that with a domain that's been around a while, not something registered last week, and you've got a much stronger foundation to build on.

In short: I'd rather buy a seasoned site with decent authority and a few scars than a perfect-looking site that's brand new. Because trust takes time to build, and when it comes to online businesses, time is one thing you can't fast-track.

Backlinks

A backlink is simply a link from one website to another.

When another site links to your site, that's a backlink, and in the eyes of Google, it's like a vote of confidence. The more high-quality sites that link to your content, the more trustworthy and authoritative your site appears.

Backlinks are one of the strongest signals Google looks at when deciding which pages deserve to rank. They're like little endorsements from around the internet. Each one says, "Hey, this content is worth checking out." And just like in the real world, not all endorsements are equal.

When I'm reviewing a site, I always dig into its backlink profile using tools like Semrush or Ahrefs. I want to see who's linking to the site, how many links there are, and most importantly, whether those links are coming from reputable, relevant sources.

A backlink from a well-known site in the same niche carries real weight. For example, if a hiking blog gets links from *REI* (Recreational Equipment, Inc.) or even just respected outdoor gear review sites, that's a strong signal to Google that the content is legit. But if that same blog is getting most of its links from shady directories or unrelated gambling sites, that's a big red flag. Not only are those links worthless, they can actually hurt the site's rankings over time.

One deal I looked at had solid traffic and revenue numbers. But when I checked the backlinks, 80% of them were from a single network of low-quality blogs, all owned by the seller. It was basically a house of cards. The moment Google caught on, those links would lose their value, and the rankings would tumble. I passed.

On the flip side, I once came across a small, under-monetized gardening blog with a backlink from Better Homes & Gardens. That's the kind of link you can't buy or fake easily; it has to be earned. That one backlink told me this site was doing something right, even if the current owner hadn't figured out how to fully monetize it yet. I made an offer the same day.

A strong backlink profile also tells you something deeper: the site likely has a "moat." It's harder for competitors to outrank a site that already has dozens of high-quality backlinks pointing to it. If you've ever tried building links from scratch, you know how tough it is. Cold outreach, guest posts, digital PR... it's all time-consuming and slow. So when a site already has that work baked in, that's real value. That's years of effort you don't have to replicate.

I'm not looking for perfection, but I do want to see a natural-looking link profile. A mix of homepage links, inner-page links, branded anchor text, and contextual mentions. That tells me the site didn't just game the system; it earned its place.

So yes, backlinks go hand-in-hand with domain authority. But they also give you a glimpse into how well the site is respected within its niche and how hard it would be for a newcomer to replicate its success. When I see a strong, clean backlink profile, I know I'm not just buying traffic or content. I'm buying trust. And in the world of online businesses, trust is one of the few things that can't be copied overnight.

Competition

I always take a hard look at the competitive landscape. Because even if a site looks solid on the surface, it doesn't exist in a vacuum. It's playing on a field with other players, and some of those players are giants.

So I ask myself: Who else is in this space? What are they doing better? Can I realistically compete here, or will I just be another voice shouting into the void?

Let's say I'm looking at a niche site about personal finance. On paper, it might look great: decent content, steady traffic, some affiliate income. But then I notice it's going up against NerdWallet, Forbes, and dozens of other well-funded publishers. That's a red flag. I don't care how clever your blog posts are. Going toe-to-toe with sites that have content teams, domain authority in the 80s, and million-dollar budgets is a brutal uphill climb. In cases like that, even a good site might not be worth the grind.

On the flip side, sometimes you stumble into niches that are surprisingly open. Maybe the competition is outdated, or the content is low-effort. Maybe no one's built a real brand around it yet. I've come across sites in niches like indoor gardening, DIY crafts, or niche health topics where the bar was surprisingly low, and all it would take to win was consistent publishing and better design. That's where the upside lives.

The trick is being honest with yourself. Not just "Can I technically write better content than the competitors?" but "Can I consistently create, improve, and outrank in a way that actually moves the needle?"

Because at the end of the day, you're not just buying what the site is today. You're buying the potential to grow it tomorrow. And that depends a lot on who you're up against.

Google Algorithm Update

After I've looked at the competition and made sure I'm not stepping into a knife fight with billion-dollar brands, the next thing I check is whether the site has been hit by a Google algorithm update. This is where things can get sneaky.

Google rolls out core updates a few times a year, and when they hit, they don't tap you on the shoulder first; they swing a sledgehammer. Sites that rely on low-effort content, AI-generated fluff, or shady SEO tactics can go from hero to zero almost overnight. One month they're raking in traffic, the next they've vanished from page one.

I've seen this happen more than once. A site that looks like a rocket ship in the metrics, with sharp upward growth and great monthly revenue, turns out to have benefited from a temporary loophole in Google's algorithm. Maybe it used AI to churn out content fast, or maybe it picked up backlinks through sketchy link exchanges. The short-term numbers looked great, but the foundation was weak. And sure enough, when the next update rolled out, the rankings collapsed.

The worst part? These crashes don't always show up right away on a listing page. Sometimes a seller lists the site right after the hit, hoping you won't notice. That's why I always pull up a graph of the site's organic traffic, usually in Semrush, Ahrefs, or Google Search Console, and line it up against known update dates. If I see a sharp drop that matches a core update, that's a big yellow flag. Not an automatic deal breaker, but something I need to dig into fast.

I once reviewed a site in the health niche that looked fantastic. Revenue was solid, content was clean, and the seller claimed "everything was organic." But when I compared their traffic timeline to Google's update history, I saw a massive drop the day a quality-focused update rolled out. Turns out, most of the content had been spun or outsourced without oversight. Google caught on, and the rankings never recovered. That deal died on the spot.

The big lesson? A temporary traffic bump from gaming the system might look great, but it rarely lasts. Google has a long memory. And while you might get away with it for a while, they always catch up. What I'm looking for is resilience. Sites that have weathered updates, or better yet, gained traffic during them, are far more valuable than those that soared fast and crashed even faster.

In short, past performance can be misleading. Always check whether the traffic is built on trust or tricks. Because when the wind shifts, only one of those will keep the site standing.

Site Speed

While I'm doing all this, I also run a quick speed test. Site speed is more important than most people realize. If a site loads slowly, users tend to leave, and Google takes notice. That can drag down rankings and revenue. A fast, clean site creates a better experience and performs better in search.

Seller's Track Record

Lastly, I always take a good look at the seller themselves. The numbers might look fine. The site might check out on traffic, backlinks, and keywords. But if the person selling it has a sketchy history, that's enough to make me hit pause.

On platforms like Empire Flippers or Flippa, you can sometimes see the seller's full profile: past listings, how many deals they've done, and reviews from previous buyers. It's not perfect, but it gives you a rough idea of who you're dealing with. Are they a builder who creates solid sites and exits cleanly? Or are they a serial flipper churning out shallow, short-lived projects?

I've seen both. One seller I came across had sold six sites in two years. Looked impressive until I tracked down a couple of those buyers through forums and LinkedIn. Turns out, several of the sites had crashed within three months. Same story every time: rankings dropped, earnings dried up, and support from the seller vanished after the sale closed. That's not bad luck. That's a pattern.

There's a difference between selling a site and offloading a site. A legit seller is usually transparent, helpful, and knows the business inside and out. They can explain the traffic strategy, the monetization, the tech stack... everything. They'll answer your questions quickly and directly. These are the folks who've built something real, and selling is just part of their process, not a fire sale.

On the other hand, if a seller dodges questions, rushes the deal, or gives vague answers when you ask about a traffic dip or a backlink strategy, that's a red flag. They might be dressing up the numbers just long enough to cash out, hoping you won't look too closely.

I try to get a feel for intent. Are they trying to build something of value, or are they just flipping fast for profit? And if I can, I reach out to other buyers or even poke around online to see how previous deals turned out. It's a little detective work, but it can save you from inheriting a time bomb.

In short, you're not just buying a site; you're betting, at least a little, on the person who built it. And if that person has a trail of broken sites behind them, don't assume you'll be the lucky exception. You want to buy from someone who's passed the test before, not someone hoping you'll be their next lesson.

By the time you've worked through all of this, you'll have a pretty solid sense of whether the business is worth pursuing. Not every site will pass the test. Most won't. But the few that do will rise to the top for a reason. Those are the deals worth moving forward on.

Having the Zoom Call: What to Ask the Seller

Once a site passes your initial filters and early due diligence, it's time to move to the next stage: a live conversation with the seller. This Zoom call is your opportunity to connect the dots between what the listing shows and what's really going on behind the scenes. It's where you confirm the good, investigate the questionable, and uncover anything the numbers don't reveal.

Now, here's something most people often overlook: your first message really matters. Sellers aren't just picking the highest bidder. They're often picking the buyer they trust to follow through and take care of what they've built. So don't just say "I'm interested" and call it a day.

Be human. Be respectful. Let them know a bit about who you are, what experience you bring to the table, and what you plan to do with the business. If something about the listing impressed you, say so. Sellers notice that. A thoughtful compliment on their branding, customer reviews, or how clean their financials look can go a long way.

Remember, they're probably juggling conversations with a few buyers. The goal is to be the one they want to sell to, not just the one with a decent offer.

And as an investor, I always treat this call as a blend of business and gut instinct. The first thing I pay attention to isn't even the numbers; it's the person. Do they seem honest? Are they upfront about the challenges as well as the wins? Do they behave with integrity? If something feels off, if they dodge basic questions or seem overly polished but vague, I walk away. No matter how good a deal looks on paper, I don't want to do business with someone I can't trust. Buffett said it best: "We buy from people we like and trust. We don't want to do business with people who lack integrity, even if the deal looks good on paper."

One of the first questions I always ask is, "Why are you selling the site?" The question sounds simple, but it tells you a lot. Over the years, I've heard all sorts of reasons. Some sellers just want a lump sum of cash. Others are burned out or ready to move on to a new project. Some flip websites for a living and this is just part of their business model. But every now and then, someone's trying to offload a site because they know the business is about to hit a wall. Maybe traffic's been quietly slipping, or a Google update is coming. They won't always say it outright, which is why your other research matters so much. It reminds me of that Peter Lynch quote: "Insiders might sell their shares for any number of reasons, but they buy them for only one: they think the price will rise." If someone's selling, you need to understand why now.

Another thing I want to know is whether this site has been sold before. I ask how long they've owned it and how they acquired it. Sometimes a seller picked it up just months ago, and now they're already looking for the exit. That could be a sign they're flipping sites, which isn't necessarily bad, or it could mean the business didn't perform the way they expected. Either way, it's something I want clarity on.

Once we get into financials, I don't settle for screenshots. I want either read-only access to the platforms they use (whether it's Amazon, an affiliate network, Shopify, or something else), or at the very least, a live screen-share during our call. Screenshots can be edited. Real-time access shows me the truth. I ask to see revenue and expenses going back at least 12 months. I want to understand what's been happening month by month, not just last week's numbers.

It's also important to look beyond the topline. I ask what ongoing expenses are involved: tools, freelancers, writers, hosting, SEO services, maybe even ad spend. With smaller sites, sellers sometimes overlook little costs, not because they're trying to deceive you, but because they don't have tight bookkeeping. That's why I dig in and ask about everything tied to running the business. I've had sellers forget to mention recurring subscriptions or freelance help, which would have changed the profit picture if I hadn't asked.

Another key question: How many hours a week does it take to run this thing? Most sellers tend to underestimate. If they say five hours a week, I mentally double it to 10 hours. You're new to the site, so even simple tasks will take longer at the start. Plus, sellers often forget to count the time they've already automated, but you still have to learn how those systems work.

From there, I like to ask about marketing and traffic. Where exactly does the audience come from? Are they using SEO, social media, Pinterest, an email list, YouTube, or paid ads? I want to understand not just what's working now, but where the opportunities or risks might be. Sometimes a site is riding the wave of one traffic channel, and if that dries up, so does the business. So I ask how much each channel contributes and whether any paid campaigns are running, and if so, what kind of return they're seeing.

Then we get into the operations. I want to know what technical skills are required to maintain the site. Do I need to know WordPress? Basic coding? Can most tasks be handled through templates or tools? I also ask what systems they have in place. Is anything automated? Who's helping behind the scenes: writers, virtual assistants, contractors? Knowing the structure tells me whether I'll be walking into a machine that runs smoothly, or a mess I'll have to clean up.

Also, I ask about the handover. I want to know if the seller is willing to help with the transition and how involved they'll be. Will they provide support for a few weeks? Are they willing to document everything they do in the form of SOPs (Standard Operating Procedures)? The more documentation they provide, the faster I can get up to speed. I've had great experiences where sellers gave me detailed guides, tools, and even email templates. And I've had others where I had to figure everything out myself. You want the former.

Before ending the call, I always like to ask one final question that often reveals more than anything else: What growth opportunities haven't you had the time or resources to pursue? This is where sellers sometimes open up about low-hanging fruit. Things like untapped content topics, neglected email lists, untested products, or SEO strategies they never got around to. Maybe they've always wanted to add a digital course, or they know the site could benefit from better monetization but didn't have the bandwidth. These insights can be gold. You're looking for leverage, ways you can step in and add value fast. And if the seller is thoughtful and forthcoming here, it's often a good sign of a business with a real upside.

At the end of the day, a content site might look fantastic in a listing, but if you don't verify the numbers, understand how the business operates, and have a real conversation with the seller, you're just guessing. This is why I treat the due diligence process in two phases. First, I filter out 90% of listings early with research. Then, I use the seller call to confirm or disqualify the few that made it through. That two-step approach saves time, keeps me focused, and makes sure I'm only spending energy on high-quality opportunities.

And like anything, the more deals you evaluate, the sharper your instincts get. Eventually, you'll get to the point where you can spot a winner or sniff out a red flag in a matter of minutes. Until then, just stick to the process, stay curious, and remember: you're not just buying a website. You're buying a living, breathing business.

Chapter Seven

Judging a Book by Its Royalties: Amazon KDP Due Diligence

"RULE No. 1: DON'T lose money. Rule No. 2: Never forget rule No. 1." — Warren Buffett.

Just like with content sites, you can do a surprising amount of due diligence on a KDP (Kindle Direct Publishing) business before you ever speak with the seller. And when you do it right, you can filter out 80 to 90 percent of the listings fast, keeping your energy focused on the ones actually worth your time. That early filtering? That's your edge. That's what separates casual browsers from serious investors.

This isn't theory for me. I've built and reviewed KDP portfolios firsthand. I've seen what works, what looks good on the surface but crumbles on closer inspection, and what kinds of books quietly generate cash flow month after month.

So in this chapter, I'm going to walk you through the exact process I use when sizing up a potential KDP deal. The tools I rely on, the patterns I look for, the red flags that make me walk, and most importantly, how I think about growing these businesses once they're in my hands.

Buying KDP assets isn't about chasing bestsellers or jumping on trendy niches. It's about understanding the engine: what drives consistent royalties, how durable the rankings are, and how easily the catalog can be improved or expanded. If you know how to read between the lines, you'll start spotting real gems and avoiding the duds that are dressed up as winners.

High Content vs. Low Content Books

When I first got into buying and building KDP assets, I started, like many people, with low-content books. They're attractive from an investment standpoint: low production costs, fast turnaround times, and a simple path to generating cash flow. Journals, planners, logbooks... you can get them designed and uploaded in a matter of days, sometimes even hours. That speed-to-market makes the model appealing, especially if you're looking to test niches quickly or build a large portfolio fast.

And in the early days, it worked. I had a few titles producing solid, predictable royalties. From a pure ROI perspective, the numbers looked great. But over time, I started to notice something: the competitive moat was shrinking fast.

The barriers to entry were low, too low. New sellers were flooding the space. Many were using design templates or automation tools to churn out dozens, even hundreds, of books a month. And because these books often rely more on packaging than content, success became increasingly about who could move faster, discount harder, and rank higher in search, even just temporarily.

As an investor, that's not the kind of model I want to double down on. It started to feel like buying into a cash-generating machine with a very short half-life. Yes, the upfront costs were low, but so was the durability. Rankings would slip, copycats would crowd in, and the only way to maintain income was to keep launching new books. That's not an asset. That's a treadmill.

So I made the shift toward high-content non-fiction, and it's been a much better fit, especially from an investor's point of view.

These books take more time and capital to produce. You might pay a writer, a researcher, or an editor. But in exchange, you get something with depth. Something that solves a real problem for a real audience. You're building intellectual property, not just selling formatted paper with a nice cover.

More importantly, high-content books are harder to replicate. If I buy a portfolio of quality non-fiction books with clear topical authority and consistent sales, I know I'm not going to wake up next month and find twenty lookalikes eating into the margins. It's a more defensible position. A stronger moat.

And because these books are often based on evergreen topics, such as personal finance, parenting, health, and hobbies, they tend to have longer shelf lives. I don't need to launch new titles constantly to keep revenue steady. That makes the model more passive, more predictable, and ultimately more valuable.

The other reason I prefer high content now? It fits squarely within my circle of competence. I know how to evaluate whether a non-fiction book is genuinely useful. I know how to research the audience, validate demand, and assess quality. That gives me confidence when I'm underwriting a deal. I'm not just buying revenue. I'm buying a durable, content-driven brand with room to grow.

So while I understand the appeal of low-content books, and I still think they have their place for quick flips or testing niches, I now invest my capital in high-content books. They take longer to build or acquire, but the payoff is stronger. In this space, I'm not playing for short-term wins. I'm looking for long-term cash-flowing assets that don't need babysitting every week. High content gets me there.

With that, let's go through a step-by-step process to find a great KDP business for your next acquisition.

What to Do Before You Ever Meet the Seller

Read Listings Like an Investor, Not a Shopper

Once you've found a few promising KDP listings, the first thing to do is slow down and read them carefully. Anyone can get excited by income on paper, but if you want to buy a solid business, you've got to read with a critical eye.

Start by understanding the basics: how many books are actually in the catalog? A business with ten well-performing titles is often far stronger than one lucky bestseller. Then look at how the revenue breaks down. Is the income coming from Kindle downloads, paperback sales, Kindle Unlimited pages read, or print-on-demand? This gives you a sense of how diversified the cash flow is.

You'll also want to get a feel for how the books are being produced. Does the seller write everything themselves, or do they use ghostwriters? That matters for how the business runs day to day and how much creative control you'll inherit.

While you're at it, pay attention to the niche they're operating in and how focused their keyword targeting seems to be. Are they publishing across random topics, or do they seem to have a clear lane?

One of the most important things to examine is how the income has trended over time. Don't just look at last month or the last 30 days. Zoom out and study the longer-term trajectory. Has revenue been steady? Climbing? Fading? Momentum matters, and you want to see consistency.

Also, pay close attention to pricing. Are the books priced appropriately for their genre? Do the prices feel consistent and competitive with similar titles? You can find potential opportunities to increase the price after the acquisition.

Reading listings like an investor means setting emotions aside and thinking like a detective. The listing may not have all the details above. In that case, simply note down the questions you want to ask the seller later.

Use KDP Tools to Verify the Data

Once a KDP listing grabs my attention and feels like it might have legs, that's when I start digging in, not emotionally, but with data. But before I touch a single tool, I always send a message to the seller asking for all the Amazon book links included in the sale. Not just the one or two they highlight in the listing, but the entire catalog.

That step alone can reveal a lot. Some sellers only showcase their top performer, the book that's riding high in the rankings and pulling most of the revenue. But I want the full picture. What am I really buying here? One hit? Or a portfolio of books with staying power?

Once I've got the links in hand, I fire up my tool stack: Publisher Rocket, Book Beam, and KDP Spy. Each one has its strengths, but together they give me a much clearer window into how the books are performing, and more importantly, why they're performing the way they are.

Historical BSR (Best Seller Rank)

First, I look at the historical BSR, or Best Seller Rank. This is one of the clearest indicators of how well each book has sold over time. Not just in a good week or during a one-time promo push, but across the long haul. It's like reading the heartbeat of the book.

BSR is updated hourly by Amazon and reflects how a book is performing compared to every other title in its category. Lower numbers are better; a BSR of 1 means you're the top seller in that category at that moment. But the real insight comes when you zoom out and look at how that rank changes over weeks or months.

I want to see if the book is consistently holding ground. A BSR that hovers between, say, 5,000 and 8,000 in its category over six months? That's rock solid. It tells me the book is moving copies every day, not just catching a lucky break. That kind of consistency often reflects a strong niche fit, solid reviews, and a well-optimized listing, all signs of a book that has found its market.

But if I see a book that had a BSR of 1,200 one month and then slowly drifted to 40,000 or 60,000? That's a different story. It might have hit the charts thanks to a launch campaign, steep discounting, or a spike from paid ads, all of which can make the book look hotter than it really is. The question becomes: What drove that initial success, and can it be repeated?

I once looked at a deal where one book's BSR had dropped from 3,000 to over 70,000 in three months. When I asked the seller, they admitted they'd done a free promo to juice downloads, followed by a heavy burst of Facebook ads. Sales spiked, but once the ad budget dried up, so did the revenue. There was no organic demand. Just borrowed attention.

On the flip side, I bought a low-content book once that never cracked a super low BSR. It hovered around 15,000 to 20,000 in its niche, but it stayed there. Month after month. And because it was evergreen (a planner), it kept selling like clockwork without much effort. That quiet consistency ended up outperforming several "hot" books I passed on that fizzled after the launch.

So when I'm analyzing BSR, I'm not just asking, "How well did this book sell at its peak?" I'm asking, "What's the trend? What's the real level of interest here? Is it holding up over time?" A strong, steady BSR tells you the book has found its audience and is delivering enough value for people to keep buying, and that's what you want in a durable KDP asset.

Estimated Monthly Sales

Then I turn to estimated monthly sales. While these numbers aren't gospel, they're incredibly useful for pressure-testing the seller's claims. Tools like Publisher Rocket or Book Beam estimate sales based on a book's BSR. They look at how books in similar ranks have performed and make an educated guess.

Now, these are estimates, not accounting records. They don't know if the author ran a promo last week or bundled the book into a box set. But over time, they paint a useful picture, especially when you're comparing them to what the seller says.

Let's say the seller claims a particular book is making $1,000 a month. You run the BSR through Publisher Rocket and see an estimated 30–40 sales per month, which, depending on the book's price, might be closer to $200 or $300. That's a pretty big gap. Now, there could be a reason for the difference. Maybe the book has a high royalty rate, or maybe the seller includes paperback and audiobook income in that number. But you need to ask. That mismatch is a prompt for a deeper conversation, not something to gloss over.

On the other hand, if the estimate is $800 and the seller claims $1,000, that's close enough for me. I don't expect the numbers to match to the penny, but like I always say, they should rhyme. If they don't, someone's either exaggerating or missing something, and either way, you've got more digging to do.

The other thing I look for with monthly sales estimates is consistency. I don't just want to see that a book sold well once. I want to know it's selling now and has been selling for several months. Because a one-hit wonder might pad this month's earnings, but it's not going to keep the lights on next quarter. I'm looking for a backlist with depth, not just one book carrying the whole load.

The goal here isn't to catch sellers lying. It's to cross-check claims and get a realistic view of what the business actually earns, not what it once earned at its peak. These estimates help ground the story in data, so you're not just buying a dream; you're buying a business that adds up.

Catalog Concentration

From there, I dig into what I call catalog concentration, basically how the revenue is distributed across the books in the portfolio. This is one of those things that doesn't get talked about enough, but it can tell you a lot about how stable (or shaky) the business really is.

If I see that one book is bringing in 80–90% of the total revenue, that's a red flag. It doesn't mean the deal's off, but it does mean I'm buying something with a single point of failure. If that one title slips in the rankings, gets a negative review bomb, or Amazon tweaks its algorithm, the entire income stream could drop overnight. It's like a restaurant that only has one good dish. If the chef messes it up, the whole night's ruined.

I've reviewed KDP portfolios where one book was a breakout hit, earning $3,000 a month, while the rest of the catalog barely made $50 combined. On paper, the revenue looked strong, but it was built on a single pillar. That's fragile. And if the seller can't give a clear plan for diversifying or protecting that top title, I start thinking about risk-adjusted returns, not just revenue.

Now contrast that with a catalog where five, ten, or even fifteen books each bring in a few hundred dollars a month. That's a different story entirely. It's not just more stable; it's more scalable. If the income is spread out, it usually means the seller understands their niche, has built a repeatable content process, and isn't relying on lightning striking twice.

One deal I did was a low-content brand with about 20 books, mostly planners, journals, and habit trackers. None of them made more than $300/month, but together they added up to consistent, passive revenue. Even better, the earnings held steady across seasons, because no single title was driving the whole engine. That kind of setup gives you breathing room and options. You can improve underperformers, build on what's working, or test new ideas without worrying that one misstep will tank the business.

So when I analyze catalog concentration, I'm not just asking, "How much is this site making?" I'm asking, "Where is it making that money and how exposed is that revenue to changes I can't control?"

The more balanced the income across the portfolio, the more confident I am that I'm buying something resilient, not just something hot.

Keyword Ranking

Then comes keyword research, and this is where things start to get really interesting, and where a lot of the upside (or risk) hides in plain sight.

I want to know exactly which keywords the books are ranking for, how competitive those keywords are, and whether people are still searching for them. Because keywords are the front door to your KDP business. They're how readers discover your books in the first place. If you're not showing up in searches that matter, you're invisible. You can find the keyword info from the same tools like Publisher Rocket and Book Beam.

Let's say a book ranks for something like "best intermittent fasting plan." That's promising. It's a high-intent keyword. Someone typing that in is likely looking for answers, maybe a guide, maybe even a product recommendation. But I'm not stopping there. I'll use Publisher Rocket or Book Beam to check monthly search volume, competition, and most importantly, who else is ranking.

If I see mostly indie authors with average covers and titles that look like they were thrown together in Canva, that's a green light. It tells me this niche is working, but not saturated with heavyweight players. I might even see a clear path to improving the listing: a better title, stronger subtitle, upgraded description, a more polished cover. In short: there's room to win.

But if heavy hitters like Penguin Random House, Men's Health, and well-known influencers with massive email lists dominate the top search results, I'll be much more cautious. Competing with major publishers is like trying to outrank Nike on the keyword "best running shoes." You can try, but it's a steep hill to climb.

I also want to know if the search volume is evergreen or trendy. Some books rank for keywords that are flavor-of-the-month, maybe tied to a diet fad, a news event, or a social media trend. That's fine if you're flipping books fast and know how to play that game. But if I'm buying for long-term income, I want stability. Keywords that people were searching for last year, this year, and will probably still be searching for next year. Things like "meal planner for busy moms" or "beginner strength training at home." They may not spike, but they rarely crash.

This step is where you start separating the books that are lucky from the books that are strategic. If a seller hits a ranking once and rides the wave, that's not the same as having a strong keyword foundation and consistent search visibility. I want books that are discoverable and will stay that way.

So yeah, keyword ranking isn't just about where the book sits today. It's about understanding the strength of the position, how durable it is, and how much room there is to improve or expand. When you get that part right, you're not just buying royalties; you're buying discoverability. And that's what keeps the cash flowing month after month.

Category Placement

I also look at the category placement. Some sellers game the system by ranking in obscure, low-competition categories just to earn the "Best Seller" badge. It looks good on the listing, but it doesn't always translate into real sales. Tools like Book Beam help sniff this out quickly.

Think of this whole process like running a stock through a screener. You're not pulling the trigger yet; you're just filtering. You're stress-testing the business before you get too excited about the headline numbers. These tools help you see beyond the lipstick and find out what's actually under the hood.

And when you get good at this? You can knock out 80–90% of weak listings in less than an hour and spend your energy chasing only the ones with real, long-term potential. That's the edge you want in this market.

Check the Quality of the Book (Don't Skip This)

This might sound obvious, but you'd be surprised how many investors skip reading the actual books. It's easy to get caught up in royalties and rank charts, but at the end of the day, you're not just buying cash flow; you're buying products. Real books that real people are paying to read.

So before you even think about making an offer, go buy the books yourself. Download the Kindle version or order a paperback. Don't just glance at the cover or skim the first few pages. Flip through them like a real customer would.

Here's what I always do. First, I read the book. Start to finish, or at least a solid sample. If the content feels lazy, confusing, or rushed, that's a red flag. Sure, the books might be selling now, but Amazon has every incentive to keep high-quality content ranked high and push the low-effort stuff down. You're buying intellectual property. And if the product itself is weak, the whole business sits on shaky ground.

After reading the book, I always take time to dig into the reviews, and I don't just skim the five-star ones. The real insight usually lives in the 1- and 2-star reviews. That's where readers tend to be brutally honest. I've seen plenty of KDP businesses that looked rock-solid on paper, with consistent income and healthy profit margins, but the negative reviews revealed the cracks. Sometimes it's sloppy typos or formatting issues. Other times it's something more serious, like recycled content or even plagiarism. One bad review isn't the end of the world, but if you see a pattern of the same complaints, that's a red flag you can't ignore.

Then take a closer look at the review profile as a whole. It's not just about how many reviews there are; it's about the quality and authenticity. A strong portfolio usually has a steady stream of organic feedback, with an average rating of 4.5 stars or higher.

If reviews look too polished or too frequent, it's worth asking whether they were incentivized or manipulated.

I also look for signs of fake reviews. It's not unusual in this space to see inflated star ratings or suspiciously generic feedback. Tools like FakeSpot can help you spot this. They're not perfect, but they give you a decent read on whether the reviews are legit or artificially padded.

Bottom line: if the books aren't good, the business won't last. Customer reviews are like a window into product quality, and they'll tell you more than any spreadsheet or seller summary ever will. Don't gloss over this step. It's one of the simplest, most revealing parts of the entire due diligence process.

Having the Zoom Call: What to Ask the Seller

Reason for selling

Once a listing passes my initial filters (the numbers look credible, the books are solid, the keyword and BSR data line up), that's when I schedule a Zoom call with the seller. This is where the real insights start to come out. The stuff you won't find in a spreadsheet or listing description.

I treat this call less like an interview and more like a reverse due diligence session. I'm trying to fill in the human gaps behind the business: the decision-making, the strategy (or lack of it), and how the machine was actually run day to day.

I always start by asking about their background and why they're selling. Simple question, but the tone and delivery usually tell you more than the answer itself. If the seller stumbles, gives vague responses, or dances around the real reason, that's a flag. On the other hand, if they're clear and direct, like saying, "I'm moving into coaching," or "I've taken it as far as I can and want to free up capital," that builds confidence.

Production Process

Then I dig into the production process. I want to know who actually created the product. Not just who clicked "publish" on KDP, but who wrote the content, designed the covers, handled formatting, editing, outlining, keyword research... all of it. Was it a solo effort? Did they work with ghostwriters? Use freelancers? AI tools? An agency? I want to understand the inputs, because those determine how replicable or scalable the operation really is.

For example, if the seller wrote all the books themselves, I know I'm going to need to build a new content pipeline to maintain or grow the catalog. That's fine, but it affects how I value the business. If they used a team of writers, editors, and VAs who are still available, I might be buying not just content, but an entire publishing system I can keep running post-acquisition.

I once got on a call with a seller whose listing looked great on paper: strong royalties, evergreen niche, solid keyword rankings. But on the call, it became clear he didn't write a word of the content. He'd used an AI tool, lightly edited the output, and outsourced the rest. The reviews were decent for now, but the moat was paper-thin. I passed.

Another seller I spoke with had published under a personal pen name and had built a small but loyal email list. They had documented SOPs for writing, editing, and launching each book, and a freelance team that was available to continue. That deal was a no-brainer. I moved quickly.

So this call isn't just about confirming what you already know. It's about uncovering what the listing doesn't show. The quality of the systems. The integrity of the process. The motivations behind the exit.

Smart questions don't just help you avoid bad deals; they help you spot great ones. These deals feature strong fundamentals, repeatable processes, and unrealized upside potential. That's where the real value live, and most of the time, you'll only find it by having a real conversation.

Financials

Once I've gone through the product and the process behind it, I move into the financials. This part is always a little trickier with KDP, because unlike platforms like Stripe or Google Analytics,

Amazon doesn't offer read-only access to the dashboard. So you can't quietly verify royalties on your own. At least, not the way you might with a content site or e-commerce business. But that doesn't mean you're stuck relying on screenshots and trust.

Instead, I always ask the seller to do a live screen share while we're on Zoom. I want them to walk me through the actual KDP backend in real time. I'm not just looking at the topline royalty number. I want to see how the seller spreads those earnings across the catalog, how those earnings have trended over the past 12 to 24 months, and how the revenue breaks down by format and region. Screenshots can be edited. But a live walkthrough, with me asking questions and the seller clicking through tabs? That's much harder to fake. You get to see the truth, or at least something much closer to it.

What I'm really after is a clear picture of how consistent the income is. If the numbers show steady or growing revenue, with healthy sales across multiple books and formats, that's encouraging. But if everything's propped up by one breakout title, I know I'm looking at a more fragile business. I'll ask for a royalty breakdown by title so I can see how concentrated the earnings are. One book carrying 80% of the load might be fine in the short term, but it raises questions about sustainability. It's a very different bet than a portfolio where earnings are spread across five or ten solid performers.

Advertising is another area where I press for clarity. Some sellers are running Amazon ads aggressively to fuel their royalties, and that's not necessarily a problem. But I need to understand how much they're spending, what kind of return they're getting, and who's actually managing the campaigns. If they're spending thousands to make thousands, and margins are razor-thin, then the business might not be as profitable as it looks. And if they're using an agency or a freelancer to handle ads, that's an added cost and potential risk I'll need to factor in.

We also talk through any other ongoing costs, such as ghostwriters, editors, cover designers, keyword tools, formatting software... all the little pieces that make the machine run. These don't always get mentioned in the listing, but they matter a lot when you're calculating true profit. I've seen deals where the seller was clearing $4,000 a month, but once you factored in ad spend, writer costs, and tools, they were really walking away with more like $1,200. Still profitable, but not nearly as attractive as it looked at first glance.

At the end of the day, this part of the process is about cutting through the noise and getting a clear view of what the business actually earns, not what the seller wants it to earn, or what it could earn if everything breaks right. I want to understand how it performs now, how stable that income is, and what it'll take to maintain or grow it once I take over. Because as much as we all like potential, I invest in what exists today. The upside is great, but it has to come on top of a foundation that actually holds up.

Operating Model

After getting a clear read on the financials, I shift the conversation to the team behind the business, if there is one. For a lot of KDP sellers, it's a one-person show. They handle everything from writing to formatting to cover design themselves. That's fine, but it comes with limitations. It usually means the business is closely tied to the seller's personal time and effort, which makes it harder to scale and hand off cleanly.

But when there is a team involved (writers, editors, cover designers, maybe even a VA running keyword research), that's when I lean in and start asking questions. I want to understand how the operation is set up. Do they have documented processes? Are there standard operating procedures in place for producing and publishing new titles? Or is everything living inside the seller's head?

This matters more than most people think. A seller with a real system, even a lightweight one, is miles ahead of someone who's just winging it. If I'm buying the business, I'm also inheriting the work of keeping it alive and ideally growing it. Having a plug-and-play structure in place for launching new books is a huge advantage. It shortens the learning curve and gives me the confidence that I can continue producing quality content without starting from scratch.

I also ask the seller if their freelancers or contractors are willing to stay on after the sale. A lot of times, the answer is yes, especially if those folks were hired through Upwork or another freelance platform. But I want to know before I commit. If a ghostwriter or designer was key to the brand's voice or look, losing them could mean starting over. That adds cost and risk.

In a recent deal I looked at, the seller had two ghostwriters who had worked with them for over a year, a dedicated editor, and a cover designer who turned around projects in under 48 hours. They had SOPs for outlining, writing, formatting, and publishing, all saved in Google Docs. It wasn't fancy, but it worked. And every one of those freelancers was willing to stay on post-sale. That setup made the deal significantly more attractive, because I wasn't just buying content. I was buying a functioning publishing engine.

So when we talk about the team, I'm not just looking for names. I'm looking for structure, reliability, and transferability. Because after the money changes hands, someone's still got to run the playbook. And if that playbook is well-documented and the team is ready to run it again, you're not just buying a book catalog; you're buying momentum.

Workload and Transition

Next, I focus on the workload and transition, because even the most promising deal can turn into a headache if you're not prepared for what it actually takes to run the business.

I ask the seller how many hours per week they're currently spending, not just maintaining the business, but actively growing it. That includes tasks like managing Amazon ads, outlining or reviewing new books, communicating with freelancers, tracking royalties, and tweaking listings. I want a real sense of the time commitment, not just a vague "couple of hours a week" answer, which often glosses over the actual effort involved.

And I go into the call knowing that my time investment will probably be higher, at least for the first couple of months. That's just the nature of taking over a new system. Even if everything is running smoothly, there's still a learning curve. You're getting familiar with the niche, the catalog, the team, the tools. I typically assume I'll need to spend twice as much time as the seller in the beginning, and then taper down once I get my arms around the business.

Another thing I ask about is whether the seller is still actively publishing new books or if the catalog has gone quiet. If they haven't launched anything in six months, that's not necessarily a deal breaker, but it changes how I think about growth. A fresh pipeline means momentum. A stale catalog means I'll need to fire things up again, which takes both time and capital.

Finally, I get clear on the transition plan. Is the seller willing to help onboard me after the deal closes? How long will they be available for questions? A week? A month? Just one call? These details matter more than most people realize. Even the best-documented business has quirks, and being able to hop on a call or shoot over a question during those early weeks can make the transition much smoother.

I also ask if they're willing to introduce me to any key freelancers (ghostwriters, editors, designers) who have been part of the process. A warm handoff can save a ton of time and preserve continuity, especially if those people have experience with the brand's tone and expectations. In a deal I did last year, the seller even offered to record a few walkthrough videos showing how they structured outlines and keyword research. That kind of gesture might not show up on a balance sheet, but it's worth its weight in gold during the handover.

The goal here isn't just to buy a revenue stream. It's to take over an engine that I can operate, understand, and eventually grow. And that starts with knowing what I'm walking into and having the right support in place for the first leg of the journey.

Purchase Agreement

I will discuss more details on this later in the book, but one of the most important steps I take is making sure the purchase agreement includes a verification window during the escrow period. This gives you a little breathing room to confirm that the earnings are real and match what was promised.

This part isn't just a nice-to-have; it's critical. Once the assets are transferred, I typically have about one to two weeks to observe the account and make sure it performs the way the seller said it would. That means checking royalty dashboards, seeing daily sales come through, and verifying that the books are actually earning, not just coasting on outdated claims.

Let's say the seller told me the portfolio earns $5,000 a month. That should roughly translate to around $1,200 to $1,500 per week. So if I log in and see just $100 roll in during that first week, that's a major red flag. Maybe it's a fluke. Maybe it's a seasonal dip. But more often, it's a sign that the revenue claims were inflated, or worse, the earnings had already dropped before the deal was made and the seller didn't disclose it.

That's exactly why I push for protection clauses in the contract. If I've structured the deal properly, with clear performance expectations and a contingency period baked into the escrow terms, I can walk away before the funds are fully released. I don't have to go to court or beg the seller for a refund. The money is still sitting in escrow, and I have a legal out if things don't line up.

This kind of clause isn't about being difficult or distrusting. It's about protecting your downside. Deals can fall apart after transfer, especially in digital businesses where so much depends on intangible factors like rankings, royalties, or ad performance. Having a built-in verification period gives you the space to catch any surprises before you're locked in.

So before I sign anything, I make sure I'm not just buying the numbers I saw. I'm buying the numbers I can actually verify. That's the difference between a smart acquisition and an expensive lesson.

All of these questions aren't just about getting answers; they're about getting a feel for the business itself. You're not just buying numbers. You're stepping into someone else's system, and your job is to figure out if that system will keep running once they're gone.

Red Flags That Make Me Walk Away

Over time, I've learned to trust my gut and move on quickly when something doesn't feel right. There are a few patterns that almost always signal trouble.

If I see a sudden spike in revenue with no clear explanation, I dig deeper. Often, it's the result of a short-term promotion or a burst of ad spend, something that isn't sustainable. That said, there are legitimate seasonal bumps. Around November and December, for instance, it's perfectly normal to see a surge in sales as people buy books for holiday gifts. But outside of that, unexplained spikes are a red flag.

Another big warning sign is over-reliance on a single title. If one book is driving most of the revenue, especially in a highly competitive niche, the entire business becomes fragile. One algorithm change, a new competitor, or a drop in rankings can knock the legs out from under it.

I also steer clear if the seller can't verify where the content came from. If they can't tell you who wrote the book or where they got the rights, that's a legal risk I'm not willing to take.

And finally, I'm especially cautious with AI-generated or low-effort content. You can spot a lot just by reading the book yourself and checking out the low-star reviews. If readers are pointing out generic writing, bad formatting, or inconsistencies, chances are the content was slapped together. That kind of business doesn't last.

In deals like these, the red flags are rarely hidden. They're usually in plain sight. You just have to know what to look for and be willing to walk away.

Growth Levers After You Buy

This is the part I really enjoy: growing the business after the deal is done. And honestly, this is where experience matters. I've scaled KDP portfolios not by chasing trends or overhauling everything, but by sticking to consistent, boring execution.

The first and most important lever is optimizing Amazon Ads. If you learn just one skill to boost profitability, make it this one. Well-run ads can take a strong performer and make it even better, or breathe life back into a book that's underperforming. I'm always testing different combinations of ad copy, bid strategies, and keywords to find what works. I keep a close eye on ACoS (Advertising Cost of Sales), and I'm quick to cut anything that isn't delivering. The winners? I scale those slowly and deliberately. Ads aren't magic, but they do compound if you manage them well.

The second big lever is launching new books. A healthy KDP business doesn't just rest on its back catalog; it grows. I use keyword tools like Publisher Rocket, Book Beam, and KDP Spy to spot overlooked, high-potential keywords. That's the foundation. From there, I build book titles around what readers are already searching for, not what I think they want.

If I'm not writing the books myself, I make sure to create strong outlines and hire ghostwriters who can deliver quality work. On a separate note, I am writing this book on my own without a ghostwriter because I'm mostly telling my own experiences. Anyway, once the manuscript's ready, I run simple but effective launch campaigns. That includes emailing your subscriber list (if you've built one) and offering free copies in exchange for honest reviews. I also promote the launch on social media and tap into platforms like BookBlaze and Pubby to help gather early feedback. Just remember: platforms like Pubby operate on a point system, so it's smart to start reviewing other books ahead of time to build up credit before your own launch.

Every new title adds to your monthly cash flow. And if you're publishing into evergreen niches, topics that don't go out of style, those royalties can keep coming in for years. Growth doesn't have to be flashy. It just has to be consistent.

Chapter Eight

Intrinsic Value and Margin of Safety: The Buffett Math for Online Businesses

"**P**RICE IS WHAT YOU pay. Value is what you get." — Warren Buffett.

If you've spent any time in the stock market, you've probably heard the term **intrinsic value**. It's the core idea behind value investing, and it's the lens Buffett uses for every investment he makes. You figure out what something is actually worth, then buy it for less than that. That gap between price and value? That's your margin of safety.

Well, the same principle applies when buying an online business, whether it's a content site or an Amazon KDP portfolio. The only difference? You're not buying a piece of a big public company with quarterly earnings reports and Wall Street coverage. You're buying a small, privately owned business, often run by a solo operator, and you have to do all the work yourself to figure out what it's worth.

I've been investing in online businesses for a while now, and I can tell you this: if you can get good at valuing these deals, you'll have a serious edge. Most people rely on rough multiples or gut feelings. But if you come in with Buffett's mindset, looking at future cash flows, risk, and sustainability, you'll avoid overpaying and spot the underpriced gems others miss.

Valuing Public Stocks vs. Private Online Businesses

Let's start with a simple question: how is buying an online business different from buying shares of a company like Apple or Coca-Cola?

The truth is, they may both be investments, but they live in two totally different worlds.

When you buy a public stock, you're stepping into one of the most transparent markets on Earth. You've got SEC filings, analyst reports, quarterly earnings calls, and reams of audited financials. You can buy or sell at the click of a button. Valuation tools like discounted cash flow models, P/E ratios, and comps are widely available, and every number you need is just a Google search away.

But when you're evaluating a private online business, say, a content site or a KDP portfolio, you're flying without radar. There are no analyst reports. No third-party research firms. The numbers come directly from the seller, often unaudited, and you have to do your own digging. There's no instant trade. You have to talk to the owner, ask the right questions, negotiate terms, sign legal agreements, and hope you're not missing something hidden beneath the surface.

Now, here's the good news. All of that extra work is actually where the opportunity lies. Public markets are efficient. Everyone is looking at the same data, and prices usually reflect that. Private online businesses, on the other hand, live in a messy, inefficient corner of the market. And when a market is inefficient, that's where value investors thrive.

A Simple Way to Understand Intrinsic Value

Let's keep this really simple: intrinsic value is what a business is worth based on the cash it will earn in the future.

"The value of any stock, bond or business today is determined by the cash inflows and outflows–discounted at an appropriate interest rate–that can be expected to occur during the remaining life of the asset." — Warren Buffett, 1992 Shareholders' letter

When you buy a business, whether it's Apple stock or a website that earns affiliate income, you're not just buying the income it makes today. You're buying the future stream of cash that business will generate over time. You estimate the future cash flows, apply a discount rate to reflect the risk, and you get a present value. That's the theoretical price you should be willing to pay.

Now, in theory, DCFs are great. But when it comes to small online businesses, most investors don't run a full spreadsheet model. Instead, they use something more practical and more common in this space: Seller's Discretionary Earnings, or SDE.

What Exactly Is SDE?

SDE is the most common way sellers and brokers present earnings in the online business world. It's not the same as net income, and it's definitely not just another name for profit.

Think of SDE as a more useful way of understanding how much money the owner is actually putting in their pocket each year. It includes not just the profit the business generates, but also the salary the owner pays themselves, any perks or personal expenses they run through the business, and even non-recurring or one-time costs that won't show up again next year.

Let's walk through an example. Suppose a seller reports $50,000 in net profit, but they also pay themselves a $30,000 salary. On top of that, maybe they wrote off $5,000 in personal travel, had a $3,000 legal expense last year that won't happen again, paid

$2,000 in interest on a business credit card, and logged $5,000 in depreciation.

When you add all of that back, the total SDE comes out to $95,000. That's the number you'll see on a listing. And that's what most people use to apply a valuation multiple, say, 30 times monthly earnings, to come up with the asking price.

But here's where you need to be careful. In the public stock market, net income already includes things like the CEO's salary. That's because you're investing in a business that already has a full team running it. In the private world, SDE assumes you'll step into the owner's shoes. It assumes you're going to run the business yourself, or at least handle the tasks the seller is currently doing.

So what happens if you want to make the business passive? If you're planning to hire someone else to run it, you'll need to subtract that cost from the SDE. Let's say the business shows $95,000 in SDE, but you'd need to hire a virtual assistant or manager for $25,000 a year to do what the current owner is doing. In this case, your actual earnings (what becomes your net income) would drop to $70,000.

That's the number you should use if you're trying to compare the investment to a public stock or run a DCF analysis. Because that's the amount of money you'll actually earn if you're not handling daily operations yourself.

Why Understanding SDE Matters

At the end of the day, when you buy a business (any business), you're asking two questions: How much money will I make? And how long will it take to earn back my investment?

SDE helps you answer the first. Most sellers will list their business based on a monthly or annual SDE, then apply a multiple, something like 30x monthly earnings, to determine the asking price. So if a content site is earning $3,000 per month in SDE, it might be listed for $90,000.

But don't stop there. You still need to dig deeper. Is that SDE truly passive, or will you be working 10–20 hours a week to maintain it? Will you need to hire help? Are the add-backs real and fair, or are they stretching the numbers to make the business look better than it really is?

Buffett's first rule is simple: don't lose money. And his second rule? Never forget the first.

That's why getting the numbers right is everything. If you get them right, you could be buying a valuable cash-generating asset at a steep discount. If you get them wrong, you're not just overpaying; you're taking on unnecessary risk disguised as opportunity.

Why the Discount?

So you might be wondering: if these online businesses are throwing off real cash, why are they selling for such low multiple prices, especially when compared to public companies like Apple or Coca-Cola? Even after you adjust the numbers and get a clear view of SDE, the price still seems cheap.

Here's the simple answer: people see more risk and more effort involved.

These businesses are small. Their financials usually aren't audited. There are no investor relations calls or Wall Street analysts breaking it all down for you. You're the one doing the digging. And unlike buying a share of Coca-Cola, owning an online business might require you to actually do some work, or at least hire someone who will.

That might sound like a downside. And for many investors, it is, which is exactly why there is opportunity here.

This is a part of the market that institutional investors don't touch. Hedge funds aren't prowling Empire Flippers or Motion Invest. The big money stays away because these businesses are "too small to matter." But if you're a solo investor and willing to learn the ropes, you're entering a much less efficient market. And when markets are inefficient, prices can get out of whack. That's where disciplined investors, the kind Buffett would admire, can thrive.

What Drives the Multiple?

When I look at an online business, I'm not just focused on the SDE. I want to know whether the multiple is fair, and more importantly, whether it's sustainable. Some factors matter a lot more than others.

For one, the age of the business is huge. Older businesses tend to be more stable. If something's been earning consistently for three to five years, I'll pay a higher multiple than I would for a site that just started last year. Longevity builds trust.

Revenue trends are also important. Is the income going up, staying flat, or slowly fading? Everyone wants growth, so sites with an upward trajectory tend to command higher prices. A flat or declining business? That should come at a discount, unless there's a clear plan to fix it.

Then there's traffic quality. Not all traffic is created equal. If most visitors are coming from organic Google search or direct traffic from loyal readers, that's more valuable than paid traffic or random social clicks. U.S.-based traffic tends to monetize better too, especially for ad-based businesses.

I also look closely at the niche. Some topics are evergreen, like personal finance, health, or education, and tend to perform well for years. Others are trendy and burn out fast. A website about fidget spinners might have made great money in 2017, but try selling that now.

Diversification matters too. If one blog post or one book is making 80% of the money, that's a risk. You want revenue spread across many assets, so no single point of failure tanks the whole business.

And then there's how much work the business actually takes to run. Passive businesses, the kind that hum along with minimal input, get a higher multiple. If it takes 30 hours a week just to keep the lights on, the price should reflect that.

Lastly, I think about transferability. Can I step in and run this business? Or is it built around a single person's name, face, or unique knowledge? If the business depends too much on the seller, or on a specific brand that I can't easily replicate, it becomes a lot harder to justify a high price.

These are all things the market doesn't price perfectly. And that's the beauty of private online business investing. It's not clean, and it's not always obvious, but that's exactly why there are deals worth finding. Just like Buffett found hidden value in See's Candy, the smart online investor can find cash-generating businesses hiding in plain sight, simply because no one else took the time to look closer.

And here's why all of this really matters: someday, you might want to sell the business. If you're building with the end in mind (and you should be), every one of these factors we just talked about plays a huge role in how valuable your business will look to the next buyer. The more stable the income, the more diversified the traffic, the less time it takes to run, the more someone will be willing to pay for it. Just like you're looking for quality when you buy, future buyers will do the same. So the smarter you are about these things now, the bigger the payoff later.

How I Think About Margin of Safety When Buying an Online Business

"The three most important words in investing are: margin of safety." — Warren Buffett

Once I've kicked the tires on a deal and the numbers check out, I don't stop there. That's just the surface. Now I want to understand what the real earning power of the business is, not the version dressed up for sale.

First, I start adjusting the numbers to get a clearer picture. I add back any necessary expenses that were conveniently "forgotten." Things like ad spend, contractor costs, software tools, hosting. You'd be surprised how often sellers leave these out, either on purpose or because they genuinely didn't track them.

Then I smooth out seasonality. If November is always a blowout month because of Black Friday, I ask: "Is there a good reason to believe that'll keep happening?" If yes, and the business has a repeatable playbook that consistently drives those sales, I'll include it in the annual average. But if it was a one-time fluke, or there's no clear reason to expect a repeat, I'll pull it out. No sense in building a valuation on wishful thinking.

Next, I zoom in on the trend line. Is revenue holding steady? Going up? Or quietly slipping downhill? A flat business with strong retention might still be a good deal. But a declining one needs a lot more margin of safety baked in.

And here's the key question I always ask myself: "If I buy this and never lift a finger to grow it, how long will it take to earn my money back?"

If the answer is 24 to 30 months and the business is stable, I'm interested. That's like earning 40–50% a year on my money, which is hard to beat. And that doesn't even include any upside from improvements I might make.

But if the deal looks like I'll be grinding 15+ hours a week just to keep it from sliding backward, then I want my capital back faster, ideally within 18 months.

This simple mental model keeps me grounded. It stops me from falling in love with a business that looks pretty on paper but doesn't hold up under the hood.

Charlie Munger once said, "No matter how wonderful a business is, it's not worth an infinite price." That's how I think about every deal. I'm not looking for perfect. I'm looking for durable, reasonably priced, and with a margin of safety that lets me sleep at night.

Rule of Thumb Multiples for Undervalued Online Businesses

When I'm hunting for deals, I like to keep things simple. One rule of thumb I've leaned on for years is this: In the stock market, when a company's price-to-earnings ratio falls below 10, I start paying close attention. That doesn't mean it's automatically a bargain, but it could mean the market is either missing something or expecting too little. Either way, it's a signal worth investigating.

Now, when I look at online businesses, I use a similar filter, just with a different measuring stick. Instead of looking at the P/E ratio, I look at the multiple of the monthly SDE the business is selling for. If the asking price is under 24 times the monthly SDE, I lean in. That's the rule of thumb that I use. That's because, on paper, I can earn my money back in two years, and that's before factoring in any growth or improvements I might make. It's the kind of math that gets interesting fast.

But the best opportunities often aren't the ones with perfect numbers. They're the ones that look a little rough on the surface, where the problems are real, but fixable. Sometimes a business is undervalued not because it's broken, but because it's been ignored. Maybe the website is slow and hasn't been optimized in years. Maybe the design looks like it's from 2010, or the business has no real social media presence. Sometimes the SEO hasn't been touched, or the product pages are a mess. These things turn off a lot of buyers, but to me, they're opportunities. If the core is strong, with a good product, loyal customers, and solid cash flow, then those flaws aren't red flags. They're ways to add value, fast.

It's like finding a good house in a great neighborhood that just needs new paint and better landscaping. Most people walk away because they can't see past the weeds. But if you're willing to put in a little elbow grease, you can unlock hidden value the market has priced in as a problem, not a project.

Buffett talks about buying wonderful businesses at fair prices. I'd say, in the world of online businesses, there's also something to be said for finding "good bones" (solid fundamentals) that are hidden under a layer of dust. That's where the bargains live.

Case Study: Valuing a Content Site the Buffett Way

Imagine you're scrolling through listings on Motion Invest and come across a content site for sale. It's in the sleep health niche: evergreen, always relevant, and unlikely to be disrupted anytime soon. The seller claims the site earns around $1,200 a month in discretionary income. You adjust for a few things they left out, such as virtual assistance salary, and get $800 a month profit. The asking price? $24,000.

At first glance, that's a 30× monthly earnings multiple. For a content site, that's not cheap, but it's not outrageous either, especially when you factor in the niche and the nature of the traffic. About 85% of the visitors come from organic search, mostly in the U.S. That's high-quality, recurring traffic, which is the lifeblood of any content business. And the owner says they're only spending 2–3 hours a week on it, so it's low-effort. The earnings have held steady over the past year, which tells me it's not a flash-in-the-pan site riding some temporary trend.

When I look at a deal like this, I start by running the simple math: $24,000 divided by $800 gives me a payback period of 30 months. That's about two and a half years to earn my money back, assuming nothing improves. Not lightning fast, but not bad for a business that could run mostly on autopilot.

Then I think about risk. Are there red flags? Not really. The backlink profile is clean, traffic's been stable through recent Google updates, and there's no shady history or sudden earnings spike that looks too good to be true.

Now, here's where it gets fun: the upside. If the site doesn't already have display ads, that's low-hanging fruit. Dialing in the display ads could add another layer of revenue. And building an email list or a lead magnet? That opens the door to future monetization that compounds over time. With a little SEO know-how and some patience, I could probably improve the value of the site without sinking a ton of time into it.

To me, this feels like a fairly priced deal with room to grow. It wouldn't be a flip-and-double play, but if I were looking for a semi-passive income stream I could gradually improve, I'd give it serious thought.

As Buffett says, "It's far better to buy a wonderful company at a fair price than a fair company at a wonderful price." This might not be wonderful yet, but it's solid, and with a little work, it could get there.

Chapter Nine

The Art of the Deal (Without Overpaying)

"**Y**OU DON'T GET WHAT you deserve. You get what you negotiate."

That line holds especially true when you're buying a business. Once you've found one that makes sense (the numbers add up, the story checks out, and you've done your homework), the next step is negotiation.

Now, this is where a lot of first-time buyers get a little anxious. I get it. The word "negotiation" sounds like you need to be slick or hard-nosed. But in my experience, that's not what gets deals done. At least not the good ones.

The best negotiations aren't battles. They're conversations rooted in clarity. You're not trying to squeeze the seller dry or get some magical discount. You're buying a real business, with real income and real risks. Your job is to build a deal that protects your downside, aligns incentives, and makes sense for both sides.

Think of it this way: you're not trying to "win" the negotiation. Your goal is to structure a deal that protects your downside, sets expectations clearly, and gives you confidence moving forward. The more informed you are about the business, the market, and what could go wrong, the more confident and fair you can be at the table.

Let's talk about how to do that the right way.

Acquisition Price & Deal Structure

Price is What You Pay, Structure is How You Protect Yourself

In the last chapter, we walked through how most online businesses, including KDP portfolios, are typically priced: monthly profit times a multiple. That multiple usually falls somewhere between 20× and 40×, depending on the quality of the business. It's a simple formula on the surface, and for the most part, it works.

But here's where newer buyers often get tripped up: They focus entirely on the price and forget that the structure of the deal can matter just as much, if not more, than the headline number.

Two people could buy the exact same business for, say, $60,000. But if one pays it all upfront, and the other negotiates a staged payment over 90 days with protections tied to performance, their outcomes could be wildly different.

I've seen it firsthand. One buyer pays cash upfront, trusting the seller's word and a few screenshots. Everything looks good for the first week, then earnings suddenly drop off a cliff. Maybe the traffic was artificially inflated. Maybe the seller ran one final promo to juice the numbers before handing over the keys. Either way, the money's gone, and the buyer is left holding the bag.

Now take the second buyer, same business, same $60K price. But they structured the deal with an earnout: $30K up front, $15K after 30 days, and the final $15K after 60 days, contingent on the business hitting the same revenue targets the seller claimed during due diligence. If earnings fall short? That last payment gets reduced or held back. It doesn't protect you from everything, but it gives you leverage. It buys you time. And in many cases, it can save the deal, or at least limit your downside.

This is why I always say: price is what you pay, but structure is how you protect yourself. Especially with digital assets like KDP businesses, where much of the value is intangible. Think rankings, royalties, and relationships with freelancers. Having smart terms can be just as important as getting a good deal on paper.

Whether it's a verification period during escrow, staged payments, seller support after closing, or performance-based earnouts, the way you structure the deal is what gives you breathing room to confirm what you're buying, and to walk away if something doesn't smell right.

Buying right isn't just about finding the right asset. It's about crafting a deal that leaves you protected if things don't go exactly to plan. Because in this space, they rarely do.

Let me walk you through the most common setups.

How Escrow Works in an Acquisition (And Why It's Your Friend)

Escrow is basically a neutral holding tank for money during a deal.

Here's what that means in plain English: Instead of wiring your payment directly to the seller on day one, you send it to a trusted third party, usually an online escrow service like Escrow.com or one tied to the broker. They hold the money until both sides have done what they promised.

Think of it as guardrails for the handoff.

Let's say you're buying a content site for $60,000. You agree to pay 90% upfront ($54,000), and hold the last 10% ($6,000) in escrow for 60 days. You send the full $60,000 to the escrow service.

Once the seller transfers the domain, hosting, content, social accounts, basically everything tied to the business, you have usually 7 days to check the asset and confirm the handover is complete. Then, the escrow service releases the $54,000 to the seller.

The remaining $6,000 stays in escrow for those 60 days. Why? Because you want to make sure the business still performs as it did before the sale. No funny business. No sudden revenue drop-offs or secret sauce that turns out to be expired.

If everything looks good after that 60-day window, you tell escrow to release the final $6,000. Done.

But if something is off, say, traffic tanks or the revenue was inflated during due diligence, you've still got that final chunk as leverage. You can pause the release and work things out, or in worst-case scenarios, escalate the dispute.

Escrow gives both sides peace of mind. Sellers know the buyer has the money. Buyers know they won't get stuck holding the bag if something shady happens.

Think of it like dating before marriage. You're both showing good faith, but nobody's blindly trusting a handshake.

So if you're doing a deal, especially over $20K, always use escrow. It's one of the simplest ways to protect yourself without complicating the process.

All Cash Upfront

This is the simplest deal structure, and also the riskiest. You pay 100% of the agreed price at closing, the seller transfers the assets, and you part ways. Sellers love it because it's fast, clean, and final. They get their payday, and they're out the door.

But for you as the buyer? This is where you're walking without a net.

If revenue drops a week later, or a key freelancer disappears, or you discover something the seller forgot to mention, tough luck. You've already paid, and the leverage is gone. There's no built-in safety mechanism. No runway to verify performance. You own it now, for better or worse.

That's why, even if I'm planning to do an all-cash deal, I always use escrow, and I make sure the agreement gives me at least 7 days to review the business post-transfer. This isn't just a formality; it gives you a short window to confirm that royalties are coming in, ads are still running smoothly, and nothing's broken under the hood. If anything looks off, you have time to raise the flag before the money is released to the seller.

I'm not saying all-cash deals are bad. In some cases, they can help you win a deal, especially when the seller's looking for a quick, clean exit. But if you decide to take that route, make sure you've built in enough protection to verify what you're actually buying. Because once the money moves, so does the risk, and after that, you're on your own.

Holdback or Escrow Release

This setup works like a built-in insurance policy. Instead of paying the full amount on day one, you put down, say, 85% at closing, and the remaining 15% stays in escrow for a set period, usually 30 to 90 days. During that window, you get to monitor the business. You see how it performs under your ownership, confirm that royalties are coming in as expected, and make sure there are no nasty surprises hiding under the hood.

If everything checks out, the final payment gets released to the seller. If something's off, say, a big drop in earnings or some part of the business was misrepresented, you've still got leverage. That holdback gives you room to renegotiate or even walk, depending on how the agreement is written.

This kind of structure is especially common on deals over $50,000, and in my opinion, it's smart for both sides. Sellers who are confident in what they've built should have no problem with it. And as a buyer, it gives you just enough cushion to verify you're not stepping into a mess.

I've used this model on several deals, and it's saved me more than once, not because the sellers were dishonest, but because there are always unknowns in a transition. A holdback gives you breathing room to find those unknowns before the full check clears. In a space where most of the value is tied up in intangibles like rankings, content quality, or relationships, that buffer can be the difference between a smart buy and an expensive regret.

Earnouts

An earnout ties part of the seller's payday to how the business performs after the sale, which can be a smart move when future stability or the seller's involvement is still a question mark.

Instead of paying everything upfront, you might pay half at closing, then spread the rest out over 6 to 12 months, but only if the business hits agreed-upon milestones. That could be revenue targets, royalty levels, or even specific deliverables like helping you launch new titles or transition key relationships.

What I like about earnouts is that they keep the seller engaged. They've still got skin in the game, which can be hugely valuable, especially in deals where their knowledge, systems, or personal presence drives a lot of the business. Maybe they're the face of the brand, or maybe they're the one managing a team of writers or ad campaigns behind the scenes. In those cases, you want them to stick around, at least for a while, and an earnout gives them a financial reason to do so.

I've used this structure in cases where I wasn't entirely sure how much of the business was tied to the seller's effort. Maybe the listing looked good, but I needed more time to understand how automated it really was. The earnout gave me a way to hedge. I wasn't on the hook for the full amount unless the business kept performing.

Now, it does require some trust and clear documentation. You need to spell out the terms: what counts as hitting the target, how it's measured, and when payments will be made. But when it's done right, an earnout can align both sides and smooth the transition.

For buyers, it de-risks the deal. For sellers, it rewards them for setting you up for success. And when there's still uncertainty in the air, whether around performance, systems, or people, it's often the fairest middle ground.

Seller Financing

Sometimes, instead of borrowing from a bank, you borrow from the seller themselves. They become your lender. You might put down 60% upfront, then pay the rest later. Maybe half in six months, the other half in a year.

It's not super common, but it can work well in bigger deals or when you want to hold on to more cash early on. Sellers who have real confidence in their business are often open to it, especially if they know it's the difference between closing the deal or watching it fall apart.

There's also a tax angle. If they stretch out the payments, they might be able to spread out the capital gains over a few years instead of getting hit with a big tax bill all at once. For the right seller, that can be a pretty compelling reason to play ball.

In summary, price and payment terms are two sides of the same coin. They move together.

If you're offering all cash upfront, you're giving the seller certainty, and in return, you can usually push for a lower price. Sellers love a clean, fast deal. No waiting, no risk.

But if you're asking the seller to carry part of the deal, say you're putting down a small amount and financing the rest over time, they're taking on more risk. And they'll often want a higher price to balance that out.

Seller-Retained Equity: A Way to Keep the Seller in the Boat

Sometimes, instead of buying 100% of a business, you buy most of it and let the seller keep a slice of equity. This setup can work beautifully when the business is growing fast and the seller still believes in where it's headed. They get to cash out a big chunk now, but keep some skin in the game for the upside later.

For the buyer, there's another benefit: you're not just buying a business; you're keeping the person who knows it best around. In a way, you're turning the seller into a kind of partner consultant. They're financially motivated to help the business grow, because they still own part of it.

But, and this is a big one, you've got to put everything in writing. Define exactly what the seller's role will be going forward. Are they advising on strategy? Helping with operations? Just passively holding equity? And what does that equity entitle them to? Monthly dividends? Annual payouts? No one likes surprises after the check clears.

Also, sellers should understand that equity isn't cash. Once they're out, it can be hard to liquidate that remaining stake. There's often no open market; the only likely buyer is you, the new owner. So unless that's spelled out in your agreement, their money could be tied up for years.

Done right, this setup creates a win-win. You, the buyer, get ongoing help from someone who deeply understands the business. And the seller gets to ride the rocket a little longer, even after handing over the keys.

Why Speed Matters

Speed matters, sometimes as much as the price itself.

If you can move fast and make the process easy, that's a huge selling point. Sellers aren't always chasing the highest bidder; they're often chasing the path of least resistance. Certainty. Simplicity. A clean close. If you can offer that, you're in a stronger position to get favorable terms, even at a lower price.

Warren Buffett is the perfect example. He doesn't drag his feet. He looks at the numbers, talks to the owner, and if it makes sense, he moves.

"When we buy companies, we don't send in teams of consultants or MBAs. If it takes more than a couple of hours to understand, we're not interested." — Warren Buffett

That kind of decisiveness builds trust. It makes you the buyer sellers actually want to work with. And when that happens, you get better deals.

What's an Asset Purchase Agreement and Why It Matters

When you're buying an online business, you're not always buying the whole company. You're usually buying its parts: the domain, the website, the content, maybe the email list, maybe a few software tools or supplier relationships. That's where an Asset Purchase Agreement (APA) comes in.

An APA is a legal document that spells out exactly what you're buying and how the deal is going to work. It lays out the price, the assets included, any terms around support or training from the seller, and what's not included, which can be just as important. Think of it as the map both sides follow to make sure nothing slips through the cracks.

On platforms like Empire Flippers, most deals use a standard APA that's already baked into their Terms of Use. It's simple, and for most six-figure deals, it works just fine. There's a spot when you make an offer where you can add any special terms. Things like seller support, transition timelines, or non-competes. That box is your chance to tailor the agreement to your needs without hiring a lawyer.

But if you're doing a seven-figure deal, or if the business has a lot of moving parts, Empire Flippers might suggest a custom APA. That's where either side can bring in a lawyer to draft something more detailed. EF will review it to keep things fair, but they advise against using generic templates you find online. A SaaS business and a content site have very different needs, and the agreement should reflect that.

Flippa also gives you access to legal support through something called Flippa Legal, powered by Contracts Counsel. It's especially handy for bigger deals or when you're unsure how to structure certain parts of the sale.

Here's the big takeaway: whatever route you go, don't gloss over the details. Spell out exactly what's included: domains, email lists, content, code, suppliers, VAs, IP... the works. It avoids headaches later. Buying a business without a clear APA is like buying a house without checking the deed. It might look fine on the surface, but you won't know what you actually own until it's too late.

Legal Landmines to Watch Out For

Before you buy any online business, take a beat to look under the hood. You don't want to close the deal only to find out you just bought a lawsuit.

Start with intellectual property. Make sure the seller actually owns everything they're selling, especially the content, code, logos, and trademarks. If it's a blog, who wrote the articles? Were they ghostwritten, AI-generated, or ripped from somewhere else? If it's a product brand, is the name trademarked, and if so, who owns it?

Next, ask about any legal skeletons in the closet. Are there ongoing disputes? Past threats from competitors? DMCA takedowns? These don't always show up in the listing, but they matter. If there's a mess, you could inherit it, and that's rarely worth the headache.

Then there's compliance. Some industries, like health supplements, finance, or anything that collects customer data, come with serious rules. If the business isn't following GDPR, CCPA, or whatever local regulations apply, that's a problem. And if they're operating in a regulated niche without the right licenses or disclosures, that could turn into legal trouble fast.

None of this means you need a law degree to buy a business, and you don't need to be a lawyer to get through it, but it's smart to hire one to review the APA before you sign, especially if it's a meaningful deal, say anything over $50K. It's a small price to pay for peace of mind. A good contract won't fix a bad deal, but it can protect you from a lot of surprises. Marketplaces like Empire Flippers and Flippa can connect you to legal services.

Asset Transfer

Once the funds land in escrow, you're almost at the finish line. But before everything becomes official, there's one final window: the inspection period. This is your last shot to dig into the business before the deal closes. It usually lasts about seven days, though it's often negotiable. Many sellers are fine giving you ten or even fourteen days if you ask upfront, even if you agreed to do an all-cash deal instead of earnouts.

This stage is different from earlier due diligence. Now, you're inside the business for real. You're not just watching a screen share anymore. You're logging into the actual accounts, reviewing the raw data, and making sure everything lines up with what the seller told you. It's where you double-check the financials, confirm the traffic, and make sure the revenue sources are working exactly as promised.

During this period, you're also collecting all the assets that make the business run. That might include domain names, access to the website or CMS like WordPress or Shopify, affiliate dashboards, ad accounts, email lists, product files, documentation, and maybe even a few freelancers or contractors who've been helping keep things afloat. Everything should be turned over cleanly and completely. This is where having a clear game plan really helps. Without it, you might find yourself chasing down missing logins or overlooked assets weeks later.

As you're going through everything, take a close look at whether the numbers hold up. Are the earnings steady? Is the traffic what you expected? Are costs higher than they first appeared? And perhaps most importantly, do you now have full control of the systems that generate revenue?

It's a critical moment. The deal isn't done yet, and if something feels off, this is your chance to pause, ask questions, or even walk away. Think of it like buying a house; this is the final walkthrough. Everything should be exactly as agreed. If it is, then you're ready to close with confidence.

Final Thoughts

A good negotiation isn't about squeezing out the lowest possible price. It's about walking away with a deal that actually makes sense. One that gives you confidence in what you're getting into, a clear view of what's expected on both sides, and enough upside to justify the risk.

The price should reflect the real earnings potential and the effort it'll take to run the thing. The terms need to have your back if things don't go according to plan. Because sooner or later, something usually doesn't. And above all, you should have total clarity on what you're buying, how and when it'll be handed over, and what happens after the dust settles.

Warren Buffett has a simple rule: never buy a business you don't understand. And never agree to a deal you haven't fully thought through.

So negotiate like an owner. Make sure your downside is protected with a margin of safety. And don't sign anything until you're truly ready, not just hopeful.

Chapter Ten

Hold or Exit? Growing and Managing Your Online Empire After Acquisition

B UYING THE BUSINESS IS just the beginning.

The real work (and the real upside) starts the moment the ink dries. This is where you shift from being a deal hunter to an operator. From investor to owner. And while that transition can be a little bumpy at first, if you buy the right business, it can also be incredibly rewarding.

You're no longer just evaluating potential. You're shaping it.

In this chapter, we're going to walk through what comes next: what to do in the first 90 days post-acquisition, how to grow what you bought without breaking what already works, and how to think about your exit strategy from the very beginning. Because whether you plan to hold for cash flow or flip for a gain, the way you manage the asset today directly affects the outcomes you'll get later.

A good acquisition gives you options: you can hold and compound, reinvest profits into new books or sites, or sell at a higher multiple down the road. But those options only exist if you step into the operator role with a clear plan.

Let's talk about how to make that happen and how to make the most of the business you now own.

The First 90 Days: Don't Break the Machine

Here's the #1 rule for new owners:

"Don't break what's already working."

If something's working, don't rush in and start fixing it.

I've watched this play out too many times. Someone buys a content site or a portfolio of Kindle books. They get excited, eager to "optimize" things. So they add new plugins, change the layout, fiddle with pricing, swap out the ads. Then bam! Revenue drops, and they're left scratching their head.

Instead, your job early on is to observe, document, and learn how the business actually works. What is the baseline traffic and revenue if you don't do anything? You bought this business for a reason, so give it time to show you its full picture.

Start by digging into the content process. What's the publishing schedule? How often does new content go out, and who's behind it? If ads are part of the picture, learn how they're being managed and what's working.

Talk to the people involved. If there are writers, editors, or ad managers, get to know them. Are they good? Reliable? Replaceable? You don't have to make big decisions yet, but you should know who's on the field.

Then get organized. Sort through the logins, SOPs, analytics accounts, dashboards... all the backstage stuff that makes the show run. If you don't know where things are, you won't be able to fix them later.

Most importantly, pay attention to what not to touch. Some parts of the business are already humming. Those are the clues. Your goal isn't to reinvent the wheel; it's to understand how it rolls. Once you've got that down, then you can think about making it roll smoother, maybe even faster. But not before.

Now, It's Time to Grow

Once you've had your hands on the business for about 90 days, you should have a pretty good feel for how it ticks. The fires are out, things are steady, and now you can start thinking about growth.

But here's the key: don't try to do everything at once. That's how people get overwhelmed and waste time chasing low-impact ideas. The smart play is to pick one or two high-leverage levers and focus there. Pull hard. Get real results. Then move to the next.

If you bought a content site, one of the fastest ways to move the needle is by publishing fresh, high-intent content. Focus on topics people are already searching for: solid search volume, low competition. Write a great article, link it to relevant posts on your site, and give it time. SEO is a slow burn, but when it hits, it compounds.

While you're adding new content, don't overlook what's already there. Older posts that rank decently can often be refreshed for a nice boost. Tighten up the structure, add new sections or data, and make sure your affiliate links are pointing to the best offers. You're not reinventing the wheel; you're just making it roll smoother.

Once the content's in good shape, look at how the site makes money. Monetization is a lever that doesn't require more traffic, just smarter strategy. Maybe you're leaving money on the table with low-paying affiliate programs. Or maybe it's time to switch ad networks and see if you qualify for higher RPMs with something like Mediavine. Even testing a basic lead gen funnel can surprise you.

As you build trust with your audience, consider capturing some of that traffic with an email list. If you're not already doing this, it's a must. Just a simple opt-in form can start turning casual visitors into long-term readers and eventually customers. An email list gives you leverage. It's traffic you don't have to rent from Google or social platforms.

Finally, take a pass through the technical basics. Fix broken links, tighten up internal linking, and make sure your images have proper alt tags. These might seem minor, but together, they lift the whole site. Think of it like compound interest, small improvements stacking up quietly in the background.

Now, if you're working with a KDP portfolio, the growth levers are a bit different, but the principle is the same: find what works, then lean into it with focus.

A good place to start is Amazon ads. They can move the needle in a big way, but they're not something you want to dive into blindly. Think of them like a science experiment. Start small, track every dollar, and don't scale until you've proven what's actually profitable. It's easy to spend your way into a hole if you're not careful.

As you start dialing in your ads, take a closer look at your formats. If you're only selling Kindle versions, there's an opportunity sitting right in front of you. Adding paperback or hardcover editions can open the door to a whole new group of buyers, especially folks who prefer to hold a physical book or give it as a gift. Same content, new revenue stream.

Once your books are available in multiple formats, shift your attention to the packaging. Titles, covers, and keywords may seem like surface-level details, but they have a huge impact on whether people find (and buy) your books. A slight tweak to a title or cover design can lift conversions dramatically. These are small hinges that swing big doors.

And don't forget to mine the gold you already have. Look at your bestsellers. Can you turn them into a series? Spin off a workbook? Create a follow-up volume? When something's clearly resonating, it's almost always worth expanding. That's often where your easiest wins come from.

At the end of the day, growth doesn't come from doing a hundred things halfway. It comes from doing one or two things really well. One lever at a time, pulled with purpose.

The Power of Integration: Why Content Sites and High-Content KDP Books Are a Moat-Building Machine

When you approach online businesses as an investor, not just a hobbyist or hustler, you start to see patterns. You realize that most people are playing short games. They're chasing viral traffic, quick sales, or one-off launches. But the real upside, the kind that lasts, comes from integration. Systems that reinforce each other. Synergy. Assets that compound.

And one of the most overlooked, yet powerful combinations I've seen is this: a content site paired with high-content KDP books, both aimed at the same audience, solving the same core problems.

Let's say you've got a content site in the personal finance niche. You're writing practical blog posts about how to get out of debt, how to budget as a couple, and how to increase your credit score. Nothing flashy, just solid, helpful content that people search for every day.

Now imagine layering in a self-published book, a real one. Something like "The First 90 Days to Debt Freedom" or "How to Talk Money with Your Spouse Without Fighting." This isn't a journal. It's a thoughtful, structured guide based on the exact problems your blog is already solving in smaller pieces. You're not just repackaging content. You're expanding on it, deepening the value.

Suddenly, your blog and your book are working together. A reader finds your article through Google. They like what you're saying. They click through to learn more, and there's your book, not as a hard sell, but as the natural next step.

This is the kind of synergy that changes the economics of both businesses.

Your content site, by itself, might make money from display ads or affiliate links. That's fine. But ads are a fragile income stream; one algorithm update or traffic drop and your earnings can disappear overnight. A high-content book, on the other hand, gives you margin. It's something you control. Something that can sell on

HYUN KIM CFA

Amazon, your own site, and through your email list. Something that adds real value to your brand.

From an investor's standpoint, this matters. You're no longer dependent on one platform or one product. You've got multiple income streams, and more importantly, those streams are connected. The blog fuels the book. The book deepens the brand. The content becomes a funnel, not just for traffic, but for trust.

I've seen this play out in the parenting niche, the health space, even obscure corners like homesteading or pet care. A site that starts by sharing tips on raising chickens ends up publishing a book like "The Beginner's Guide to Raising Chickens." It's a niche product, sure, but it speaks directly to a specific person. And that person is already reading your content.

That's the kind of business that's hard to compete with. Not because the idea is groundbreaking, but because it's integrated. A competitor can publish a similar book. They can write a similar article. But if they don't have the ecosystem (the site, the audience, the email list, the long history of showing up), they're playing catch-up.

And this is where the real moat starts to form.

Every new piece of content you publish adds to your search presence. Every book you release adds credibility. Every email subscriber you gain becomes someone you can reach directly, without paying for ads or praying for algorithm mercy.

This is how you create durability.

You're not guessing what to write about next. Your audience tells you. You're not throwing books into the void. You're creating them based on real data. You're not building multiple disconnected revenue streams. You're building one brand, expressed through multiple channels.

The payoff? You don't just increase revenue. You increase valuation. Because now, if someone ever wanted to acquire the business, they're not buying a blog or a book. They're buying a system. A fully integrated, niche authority business with products, traffic, trust, and distribution, all under one roof.

This is how I evaluate digital businesses now. I don't ask, "How much are you making?" I ask, "How connected is everything?" Because connection compounds. And in a crowded market, that's the real edge.

So if you're building a content site today, don't stop at publishing articles. Think about what book only you can write for that same reader. Not a mass-market bestseller, but a focused, useful book that solves the problem your site already touches.

And if you're writing high-content books for Amazon, ask yourself: Where do these readers come from? How can I build something beyond the book — a place, a voice, a platform — so the next book doesn't start from zero?

In the end, it's not about one piece being perfect. It's about how all the pieces fit.

That's how you build a real business. That's how you build a moat. And that's how you turn simple digital properties into valuable, compounding assets.

Build Systems Early

Even if you're starting small, this is the perfect time to lay the groundwork for scale. Think long term. You don't want to build a business that needs constant babysitting. You want something that can eventually run without you, or that someone else would happily take off your hands.

It's worth repeating: you bought a business, not another full-time job. So start thinking like an owner, not an operator.

A good way to begin is by taking inventory of where your time is going. Ask yourself: "What am I doing manually that someone else could do just as well or better? What repetitive tasks could I document once and hand off? And are there tools or automations that could quietly save me ten or more hours a month?"

You don't need a full team from day one. Just start with one part-time freelancer or virtual assistant. That's often enough to free up your time for the bigger, more strategic work.

Platforms like Upwork or Fiverr make it easy to find help, often at a reasonable rate. Upwork and Fiverr both connect you with freelancers, but they take very different approaches.

Upwork works more like a traditional job board. You post what you need, freelancers apply, and you choose who to hire. It's ideal for longer-term or more complex projects where you want more control. Plus, you can pay hourly or per project. The tradeoff is that it takes a bit more time to review proposals and manage the process.

Fiverr, by contrast, feels more like an online store. Freelancers list their services as fixed-price "gigs," and you can browse, click, and buy without much back-and-forth. It's quick, easy, and great for one-off tasks that don't need a lot of customization.

If you're looking for flexibility and don't mind investing time to find the right person, Upwork is a solid choice. But if speed and simplicity are more important, Fiverr is tough to beat.

And don't get too caught up in where someone lives. Yes, U .S.-based freelancers tend to cost more, but that doesn't always mean better. What really matters is quality. Clear communication, consistent delivery, and attention to detail. That is what you're looking for, no matter the time zone.

Building systems might feel like extra work upfront, but it pays dividends down the road. The less your business depends on you, the more valuable (and enjoyable) it becomes.

Eventually, the day might come when you're ready to sell. Maybe you've outgrown the site. Maybe your interests have shifted. Or maybe it's just time to cash in and put that capital to work elsewhere.

The good news? You've already done the heavy lifting. You bought smart, ran the business with discipline, and made it more valuable. Now it's about finishing strong.

Start by cleaning up the financials. Buyers want clarity. A simple, clean profit-and-loss statement goes a long way. Show the growth. Be ready to back it up: screen shares, access to dashboards, whatever makes the numbers real and trustworthy.

Next, organize your systems. Have one central place (a doc, a dashboard, whatever works) that lays everything out: where the traffic comes from, how the business makes money, your SOPs, any contractors you work with, and what's been done so far to grow the business (plus what's still on the table).

Timing matters too. Ask yourself: "Is revenue heading in the right direction? Is the business fairly hands-off? Can a buyer see where to take it next?" If those answers are yes, you're probably in a good spot to command a healthy multiple.

Buffett once said, "Our favorite holding period is forever." But he also knows when to sell: when the money can work harder elsewhere. That's your cue too. Hold when it makes sense. Exit when it's time.

Final Word

Here's the bottom line: growing a business after you buy it isn't about doing everything. It's about doing a few important things well, consistently, patiently, and with a clear head.

The best investors don't just buy smart. They operate smart. They understand that the real wealth isn't created at the moment of purchase. It's created in the quiet, steady work that happens after.

And when the time comes to exit, they do it with discipline, not emotion.

By now, you know how to think like an owner. You know how to evaluate and acquire the right kind of business. You know how to improve it without breaking what works. And when the time is right, you'll know how to step away on your terms.

From here, it's all about taking that first step. Start small. Stay focused. Let time and compounding do the heavy lifting.

Chapter Eleven

Social Media Marketing That Moves the Needle

Fueling the Flywheel: How Social Media Drives Discovery and Growth

I CARVED OUT SOCIAL media marketing as its own chapter for a reason. In the early days of building an online business, it's easy to treat social platforms as an afterthought. Something you'll "get around to" once the site is live, or the book is published. But in today's landscape, social media has become one of the most important drivers of growth. It's no longer optional. It's a key piece of the system, and one with serious leverage if used well.

Social media isn't about chasing likes, comments, or vanity metrics. It's not about trying to go viral or look impressive. At its best, it's a discovery engine. It brings the right people, people already interested in what you're building, into your orbit. And it does that without you needing to wait on Google rankings, pay for traffic, or rely on third-party platforms to grant you visibility.

It took me a while to understand that.

Early on, I had a small content site, a growing email list, and a high-content book that I knew could help people. But the growth was slow. Then I started using Facebook and Pinterest, not randomly, not just to "be active," but intentionally. I started telling stories, sharing ideas, and talking directly to the problems my audience was already facing. That's when things shifted.

Here's what I learned: people don't buy because you posted a link. They buy because they've seen your work, heard your voice, and started to trust the way you think. Social media shortens that trust curve. It gives your brand a face, a tone, a pulse. It's how strangers become readers, and readers become customers.

That's the beginning of your flywheel. Social media drives attention to your content, your content earns trust, your products (books, services, courses, whatever you're selling) deliver value, and your audience deepens. Over time, that cycle gets stronger. But it starts with visibility.

And to be clear, you don't need to be on every platform. In fact, trying to do too much usually backfires. The smarter move is to pick one or two platforms where your target audience already spends time and then go deep. If your brand has a visual side, Instagram is a natural fit. If your niche solves long-term, evergreen problems, like fitness, wellness, recipes, Pinterest can quietly drive traffic for years. If you're willing to speak directly and show the raw side of your process, TikTok and YouTube Shorts offer a massive upside. And if your niche has strong community ties, Facebook groups still deliver real engagement.

Whichever platform you choose, the goal isn't just promotion; it's connection. A quick tip from your latest post. A behind-the-scenes look at your book research. A short story about something you've learned. These aren't throwaway posts. They're doorways. Small moments that give people a reason to stop, listen, and follow the trail back to your world.

Some will scroll past. But some won't. Some will click. Some will read. A few will join your list. And over time, that handful becomes your foundation, the ones who read every post, share your work, and stick around long enough to matter.

You can't manufacture that kind of loyalty. You have to earn it. And social media, done right, is where that earning begins.

One of the most important mindset shifts I had to make was moving away from trying to grow a "following" and instead focusing on building recognition. Not fame. Just familiarity. When someone sees your name or your content, whether it's a pin, a reel, or a post, do they know it's you? Do they feel like you're talking to them?

If the answer is yes, your presence starts to compound. Maybe slowly at first, but with substance. And substance is what drives real revenue, not just attention.

Social media isn't the business. But it is the bridge to it. And in a landscape where trust is scarce and noise is everywhere, that bridge is one of your most valuable assets.

This chapter isn't about hacks or trends. It's about strategy. Long-term thinking. How to use social platforms not to chase attention, but to direct it. How to plug them into your existing content and products in a way that multiplies their impact.

Because at the end of the day, it's not the algorithm or the platform that builds your business.

It's the trust you earn.And the story you tell.One post at a time.

Facebook: The Neighborhood Where Your Audience Already Lives

If you're working in a niche, whether it's parenting, personal finance, homeschooling, gardening, wellness, you name it, chances are your people are already hanging out on Facebook. Not everyone loves the platform, but for many niches, it's still where the most active conversations happen. Especially if you're targeting people over 30 who like to learn from others who have "been there."

And that's the key to using Facebook the right way. Don't think of it as a place to promote; think of it as a place to participate.

This isn't a billboard. It's a neighborhood. And just like in any neighborhood, people can tell the difference between someone who's there to be part of the community and someone who's there just to sell something.

I've seen this dynamic play out in real time. Years ago, one of my friends was part of a Facebook group focused on budgeting and getting out of debt. He wasn't there to pitch anything; he just answered questions, shared what worked for him, and occasionally linked to helpful blog posts he'd written. One day, he shared a simple freebie from his site. A printable budget worksheet, nothing fancy. It struck a chord. That single post led to thousands of visits and, somewhat unexpectedly, over a hundred sales of a book he'd written on budgeting.

Not because he pushed it. But because he earned the right to share it.

And that's what makes Facebook powerful when used well. You don't need to game the algorithm. You need to show up, offer value, and be useful. The more you help, the more trust you build. And trust is what turns a reader into a buyer, and a buyer into someone who spreads the word.

Now, if you've got your own Facebook Page or Group tied to your brand, even better. That's your home turf. You control the tone, the direction, the vibe. You can share content from your site, test headlines, preview book ideas, or just hang out with people who care about the same things you do.

I've seen creators use small niche groups as incubators, asking questions, spotting patterns, and shaping their next high-content book based on what the audience is already struggling with. It's market research in plain sight.

The point is, Facebook works, not as a megaphone, but as a meeting place. And if you approach it with patience and generosity, it can become one of the most reliable channels in your entire business.

People often ask, "Is Facebook still worth it?" If your audience is on there, absolutely! But only if you treat it like a community, not a commercial.

That's when the magic happens.

Pinterest: The Compounding Channel

Pinterest isn't loud. It's not trendy. And that's exactly why I like it.

While other platforms chase the latest algorithm twist or short-form craze, Pinterest plays the long game. It's not really social media in the traditional sense. It's more like a visual search engine. And that subtle difference is what makes it so powerful for content-driven businesses.

You're not trying to go viral here. You're building a library. Quietly. Consistently. Pin by pin.

Let's say you're in the productivity or wellness niche. Maybe you're writing about managing ADHD as an adult, especially in a work-from-home setting. You've got a blog post on your site that walks readers through strategies to stay focused. You've also written a book that goes deeper into that exact topic: structured routines, mental systems, tools that actually help. It's all part of the same ecosystem.

Now, take the core ideas from that blog post and turn them into a few clean, helpful pins. Think titles like "5 Focus Hacks for ADHD Brains" or "Work-from-Home Routine for Distracted Minds." Design them in Canva, keep them simple, and post them using the exact phrases your audience would search for. Not clever headlines, but keywords people actually type.

And then... let time do its thing.

Pinterest isn't about immediate traffic. It's about stacking discoverability. I still get visits (and sales) from pins I made two, even three years ago. No updates. No extra work. Just quiet, compounding attention.

It reminds me of Buffett's rule: "Someone is sitting in the shade today because someone planted a tree a long time ago." That's Pinterest in a nutshell. Every helpful pin you post is a tree. And if the content behind it actually solves a problem, that tree starts bearing fruit.

It doesn't matter if you have a following. Pinterest doesn't care. It cares about relevance and usefulness. Which makes it perfect for people who are in it for the long haul: content creators who want their work to keep working.

If you've got a solid blog and a strong book, Pinterest is how you quietly build a bridge between the two. It's slow, yes. But that's the point.

It's not a flash. It's a foundation.

TikTok and Instagram: Fast Attention, Real People, and Honest Content

Let me be upfront with you: I'm not an expert on TikTok or Instagram. I haven't built a massive following on either, and I'm not the person to teach you growth hacks or reel trends. But I am paying attention, and what I've seen from people who are using these platforms well has completely changed how I think about modern content distribution.

Because here's the truth: attention is moving fast. And if you're building an online business, especially one rooted in a content site and high-quality books, it's worth understanding how platforms like TikTok and Instagram fit into that equation.

They're not magic bullets. But when used well, they can be powerful accelerators.

Let's start with TikTok.

This platform can feel overwhelming at first. It's fast, unpredictable, and sometimes downright chaotic. But that's also what makes it special. TikTok rewards realness. You don't need professional lighting or fancy editing. You don't even need a face on camera, although that helps. What you do need is clarity, a point of view, a little honesty, and a story that helps someone feel less alone.

I've seen people take simple blog post ideas, something like "how I finally got control of my anxiety at work," and turn that into a short video with a personal anecdote, one quick tip, and a soft call-to-action at the end: "I actually wrote a book about this if you want to dive deeper. It's on Amazon. Link's in the bio."

No pressure. No big sell. Just a moment of connection.

A friend of mine built an audience by doing exactly that. He didn't have a content calendar or a strategy. He just started talking honestly about his parenting journey, what helped him, what didn't, and how he managed the chaos of early days after having a child. Over time, his TikToks started reaching people. They shared his story. They clicked his link. They found his blog. And eventually, they bought his book.

Not because he was "selling." Because he was helping, in a voice they could trust.

Now let's talk about Instagram.

While TikTok is raw and reactive, Instagram leans more into aesthetics and atmosphere. But the principle is the same: show up with something helpful, and do it consistently.

Instagram is still incredibly valuable for brands with a visual edge. If your niche lends itself to photos, design, or clean visuals (think wellness, productivity, parenting routines, food, minimalism), this is where you can give your content a heartbeat. You're not just showing a final product. You're showing how it fits into someone's life.

When I see creators succeed on Instagram, they're usually doing one of three things: They're sharing quick wins in carousel posts. They're giving "real life" glimpses behind the scenes in stories. Or they're showing up consistently in reels with the kind of content that doesn't feel produced; it just feels honest.

I've personally turned some of my blog posts into carousels on Instagram, breaking down a concept or tip over 5–6 slides. At the end, I simply say, "Want the full version? It's on the blog. Link in bio." No pitch, just a clear next step. And from there, it leads into the book, or the email list, or whatever else is part of the flywheel.

And that's how I see both platforms now. Not as a way to "go viral," but as entry points. Gateways. Little windows into the bigger thing you're building.

Not everyone who sees your content will click. Not everyone who clicks will read. But some will. And if your content site and your books deliver real value — not fluff, not filler, but honest solutions to real problems — then those few will stick. They'll follow you. Buy from you. Share your work with others. That's the momentum you're trying to create.

So no, I'm not here to give you growth hacks. I'm still figuring this out myself. But I do know that authenticity matters more than ever. And if you can show up with something worth saying, something that actually helps someone, even in a small way, then these platforms can absolutely be part of your long-term strategy.

Not the whole business. But a strong bridge to it.

In a world where everyone's chasing attention, the ones who win are the ones who keep it.And the way you keep it? You earn it.

Chapter Twelve

Conclusion

I F YOU'VE MADE IT this far, you're not just curious about buying online businesses; you're serious. You've seen how private online businesses can outshine public markets. You've learned how to find deals, evaluate them with discipline, and grow them with focus. But more than that, you've started to think like an owner. And that mindset shift is what truly separates average investors from great ones.

When Warren Buffett made the now-famous pivot from buying cheap stocks to buying great businesses, it changed everything. It wasn't just about numbers anymore. It became about quality, predictability, and people. The same lesson applies here. You're not just buying websites or royalties. You're buying systems, audiences, and compounding cash flows. And with the right mindset, these online assets can become your version of See's Candies: small, simple, and steadily throwing off cash.

Throughout this book, we've emphasized timeless principles over flashy tactics. That was intentional. The internet changes fast, but business fundamentals don't. Whether it's a content site making affiliate revenue, a KDP book earning royalties, or a SaaS tool solving a niche problem, the core question remains the same: does this business create real value for real people, in a way that's sustainable?

If the answer is yes and if the price makes sense, then you may have found a gem.

The Journey from Investor to Operator

The truth is, buying the business is the easy part. The real value gets built afterward, through systems, smart decisions, and showing up consistently. You don't have to be a world-class operator from day one. But you do need to be willing to learn. To document. To delegate. To let go of perfection and embrace progress.

This is why Buffett's best investments weren't just the ones with the best numbers. They were the ones with the best people running them. And in the case of small online businesses, you are that person. At least in the beginning.

Don't let that intimidate you. Let it empower you. Because being an operator, even a scrappy one, gives you an edge most investors don't have. You're not just betting on someone else to create value. You're building it yourself.

The Beauty of Small

One of the best parts of this game is that you don't need to hit home runs. You're not chasing the next Facebook or hoping to stumble onto a billion-dollar unicorn. All it takes is one well-run content site. One evergreen KDP book. One simple, useful software tool. That's enough to start stacking real cash flow and building real leverage.

And with every small win, you gain something even more valuable than money: confidence. You start to trust your judgment. You begin to see how this all works. That momentum is what makes the next step possible.

After that, just look at how Warren Buffett scaled Berkshire Hathaway. He didn't do it by micromanaging every business. He did it by trusting smart operators and delegating wisely. The same principle applies here. You can't do it all yourself if you want to scale your business at some point. Start with freelancers. Document your systems. Over time, you'll learn how to build a lean team that frees you up to focus on strategy, not daily tasks.

Small businesses, run well, can scale surprisingly far. Especially when you build them with systems, not just hustle.

What Comes Next

From here, the real work begins. Start by choosing one lane: content, KDP, SaaS, or ecommerce. Get to know it inside and out. Build your circle of competence. Don't try to master everything. Master one thing. Then buy your first deal. Doesn't have to be perfect. It just has to teach you something.

Run it well. Take notes. Test small changes. Build systems. Hire help. Then, if you want, buy another. Or scale the one you've got. Or exit and redeploy the capital. You're in control now.

And that's the point.

You don't need to wait for the market to reward you. You don't need to trust Wall Street or time the economy. You can create your own returns, on your own timeline, by owning and operating simple, profitable digital businesses.

Final Thoughts

Warren Buffett once said, "Opportunities come infrequently. When it rains gold, put out the bucket, not the thimble."

Right now, there's gold falling on the internet. Quiet, steady rain in the form of overlooked content sites, niche ebooks, under-loved SaaS tools, and sleepy little ecommerce brands. It's not loud. It's not hyped. But it's real.

The question is: are you ready to pick up the bucket?

Plant your tree. Run your business. Let it compound. And when the time is right, whether to hold, grow, or sell, you'll know what to do.

Thanks for reading this book and making it this far. I know your time is valuable, and I truly appreciate you sticking with me through the ideas, lessons, and real-world insights on buying online businesses.

If you found anything helpful along the way, even just one useful idea, I'd be grateful if you left a quick review on Amazon.

It doesn't have to be long. A few honest words can help others decide if this book is worth their time, and it helps me keep improving and sharing more practical tools for investors like you.

Thanks again, and I wish you all the best in your next deal.

Chapter Thirteen

Bonus: Acquisition Due Diligence Checklist

I F YOU'RE THINKING ABOUT buying an online business, you're going to need a solid due diligence process. It's easy to miss red flags when you're excited about a deal. To help with that, I've put together a **FREE** and comprehensive due diligence checklist you can use before making any purchase. It covers everything from traffic and revenue verification to spotting fake reviews and shady backlinks. Think of it like your flashlight in a dark room. You can grab it for free and use it every time you look at a new website deal.

https://buffettinvesting.com/books/buying-online-businesses/

About the author

Hyun Kim, CFA, didn't start with a trust fund or Silicon Valley connections. He built his online business the slow and steady way, working nights and weekends while holding down a demanding leadership role at a Fortune 500 firm in New York. What makes his story useful isn't just the success, but how he got there: by applying classic Buffett's investing principles to the digital world.

His goal is to show you how to invest like Buffett, but in websites, royalties, and scalable online assets. You don't need to be a tech genius or quit your job. You just need a plan, a steady hand, and a value mindset.

Rooted in Buffett-style patience and real-world experience, this book shares what actually works when you're short on either time or money but long on ambition. Whether you're just getting started or looking to scale, Jun's story will help you build digital assets that last, without losing your sanity along the way.

www.ingramcontent.com/pod-product-compliance
Lightning Source LLC
Chambersburg PA
CBHW061024220326

41597CB00019BB/3312

9 781968 387013